LOVE ME LOVE YOU

LOVE ME

The international bestseller

LOVE YOU

SAY NO TO TOXIC PEOPLE AND YES TO MEANINGFUL RELATIONSHIPS

María Esclapez

ROCKPOOL

A Rockpool book
PO Box 252
Summer Hill
NSW 2130
Australia

rockpoolpublishing.com
Follow us! rockpoolpublishing
Tag your images with #rockpoolpublishing

First published under ISBN 9788402424587 © 2022 Penguin Random House Grupo Editorial as *Me Quiero, Te Quiero*
This edition published in 2026 by Rockpool Publishing
ISBN: 9781922468208

Design and typesetting by Sara Lindberg, Rockpool Publishing
Translation by Anna Jenman
Translation edited by Kaitlyn Smith

Printed and bound in China
10 9 8 7 6 5 4 3 2 1

CONTENTS

♥

INTRODUCTION

When I first thought about writing this book, I reflected on all the relationships I'd had before experiencing true love. I wanted to write it primarily from my perspective as a professional, however I also wanted it to be informed by experiences in my own love life.

I, personally, have had a fair few toxic relationships and suffered the effects of being emotionally dependent. For a long time, I ignored the little voice inside my head telling me that things weren't working out. In retrospect, I was scared to look inward too closely, for fear of what I might find. So, sadly, I was busy silencing that voice in an effort to make it disappear.

Repressing that voice simply fed into others which sought to tear me apart. I hated myself so much that I became, for the umpteenth time in my life, my own worst enemy. While I was pouring into my partners' emotional cups, my own were running completely dry. If I could tell Dante to add one more circle to his vision of hell, it would undoubtedly be psychological suffering.

But our instincts are strong, and they don't easily relent. One day that little voice came back, and I knew it was my moment. I had to do something. I was tired of falling into the same traps over and over again. Right then, when my whole life was falling apart, in the eye of the storm, I finally summoned the strength to start working on myself.

Life dealt me numerous more blows, on both a personal and professional level, but something had begun to change – I felt different. I no longer felt ready to self-destruct with self-hatred. I had reached a new level of awareness.

I don't remember the exact moment when things changed, nor can I tell you where I was, or what was around me. But I associate it with the period when I lived in Madrid, a city that both welcomed and excited me, a place where I was also left reeling from mistreatment. There, I enjoyed life and suffered in equal measure. I met Alberto, the love of my life, who has helped me understand that even though I had probably fallen in love many times before, I was a stranger to true love before I met him.

To you, dear reader, I can honestly say that I genuinely do understand you (you can't imagine how deeply). I know that, like me, it's quite possible that you have misgivings and questions brewing inside which you don't particularly want to face. Perhaps you already suspect that the wheels are coming off in your relationship and that what you are experiencing may not be normal. It may even be all the above, and you might want to get out of the mess you're in, but you just don't know how. You've picked up this book because you can hear that little voice too, and you've finally decided to listen to it. I hope that within these pages you find the information I would have loved to have known when I was lost back then, in my darkest moments.

My intention is to get you looking inward. No matter what point you're at, it's never too early nor too late for serious introspection. I'll help you look inside, so that you really tune in, reflect, and find the answers you seek, whatever they may be.

If, a few years ago, when all I had was an unstable job that didn't make ends meet and a few codependent relationships under my belt, someone had told me I would be where I am right now, I wouldn't have believed it. I learned the hard way how to be alone and how to value myself. I cut off all those people who were only in my life to take advantage of me. I left my job and, despite not believing in anything or anyone, I returned to my hometown with a suitcase full of hope.

I decided, as I was starting down this road from scratch, to simply trust myself and my abilities, without depending on anyone or anything. And I did it. I was scared to death, but I did it. I took a couple more of those blows you never forget, but I didn't care. I carried on. I said to myself "You just keep doing your own thing, keep doing your own thing", a phrase I still tell myself from time to time. And so, the day came when all the hard work I was doing finally began to pay off. Life put people in my path who I could finally trust. I saw a brighter side of life, and I ran with it.

The María I am today is nothing like the María I used to be. It has cost me endless tears, great disappointments, and a certain amount of anxiety that I must still deal with. It has been difficult, yes, but now I have everything that I always dreamed of, and I can't help looking back and thinking that, in some way, everything I've been through taught me the importance of setting clear boundaries. Occasionally, I still recall parts of my life which make me want to cry and give myself a huge hug. Everything is different now, and although my life still isn't perfect, I have the most important pillars supporting me; my partner and my family, to whom I dedicate this book. Thank you for always being there for me, you are my safe space, my secure attachment, and the emotional stability I need when the ghosts of the past come back to haunt me.

IMPORTANT NOTES

ABOUT THE EVENTS DESCRIBED IN THIS BOOK

In this book you will find real descriptions of my own lived experiences.

You'll also be able to read accounts based on actual events from my patients' lives. The latter have been changed to safeguard and respect the privacy and identities of those involved.

Some of the situations depicted, such as WhatsApp conversations, are fictitious and belong to the Radiografías de conversaciones tóxicas por WhatsApp project *[Snapshots of toxic WhatsApp conversations]* by the same author. Those images are intended to recreate situations that can and do occur in real life.

All the names used in this book are fictitious, so any resemblance to real people is purely coincidental.

♥ 1 ♥

ON TOXIC RELATIONSHIPS AND EMOTIONAL DEPENDENCY

Before I address the more specific issues around romantic relationships, I would first like to talk about the importance of creating healthy bonds in our relationships with others and with ourselves.

From birth, and as we grow up, we gradually learn about the world and how to relate to our surroundings. What we learn, and how we learn it, forms a large part of what will determine, further down the track, how we process things, how we bond with others, and how we respond to the stimuli around us (for example, how we deal with problems). For this reason, it can be said that our personal experiences greatly influence the way that we relate, not only during clashes, but also internally, to ourselves, and to others.

AFTER READING THIS BOOK YOU'LL NEVER BE THE SAME AGAIN

One of the fundamental properties of the brain is its plasticity (meaning it's moldable). Everything that happens to us changes the way we see the world. The brain changes every second it spends processing information. For instance, if I tell you every month beginning with a Sunday contains a Friday the 13th, this becomes a new piece of information your brain processes and integrates, which in turn gives you the flexibility to change the way you look at things. Likewise, after reading this book, you will never be the same again.

This is equally applicable to relationships. Everything we're taught throughout our lifetime, whether consciously or subconsciously, influences the way we experience relationships, including the lessons we learn within the relationship itself. Human beings are like sponges, absorbing lessons about behavior, situations, words, images, ways of thinking, and attitudes. Of course, we also learn things that we don't necessarily want to learn.

Often, such life lessons are experienced as genuinely traumatic (highly charged moments of emotional intensity, negatively affecting the person's life and being forever etched on their minds). In relationships with parents, friends, or partners, any experience that causes emotional or physical suffering is traumatic because it affects the person's innermost intimate and emotional well-being. These kinds of trauma will later affect the bonds formed in relationships, which may or may not turn out to be toxic.

A toxic bond is one that causes discontent. The name says it all: something toxic is something bad or harmful to us.

The fundamental cause of such toxicity may be either down to each person in the relationship's past, and/or how it feeds into what they've learned. It is clear to me, after having witnessed and lived through many toxic bonds, that they are simply bonds resulting in behaviors. Therefore, there are no toxic people; there are just people with backgrounds combined with the lessons they've learned, who consequently display toxic behaviors.

I really want to emphasize this last point because I believe that judging someone as "toxic" not only deprives them of the ability to potentially adjust their understanding of the world and their behaviors, but it also indirectly labels them as a "bad person", something which, at least from the point of view of psychology, doesn't exist. There are no official diagnoses in the DSM (the diagnostic book used by psychologists and psychiatrists) that can designate someone as a "bad person" or a "good person". Psychology is a science. The question of being "good" or "bad" is therefore best left to individuals, their religions, and their personal moral codes.

When we talk about emotional dependence, we're talking about a need for affection and emotional attachment that involves an inability to leave a relationship even when it's causing us to suffer (the inability to leave a toxic relationship). There are moments of clarity in which the person who persists in a relationship out of dependence can clearly see that they should end it and distance themselves because it is hurting them, but they are paralyzed by fear.

On the other hand, we also have the concept of codependency, which is what we see in those who, within a toxic and dependent relationship, have the overriding need to please the other person, unconsciously motivated by the fear of abandonment; "If I give this person the very best of myself, take care of them and please them, they will never leave me". Codependent people often choose troubled individuals as partners (e.g., those suffering from mental illnesses, physical problems, and substance or gambling addictions) or who are weak in some way or other. The latter could well occur, for example, when the codependent person hears their partner tell stories of an unhappy childhood or previous relationships. The codependent person will then employ strategies to pay constant, unstinting attention to their partner. These people usually have a great capacity for endurance and tend to take on others' problems themselves, often overprotecting their partner and putting the partner's needs before their own.

According to the United Nations, "abuse can be defined as a pattern of behavior in any relationship that is used to gain or maintain power and control over an intimate partner. Abuse is physical, sexual, emotional, economic, or psychological actions or threats of actions that influence another person." That is to say, an abusive relationship is a relationship in which one of the parties exerts control over the other, or, to put it differently, where an aggressor (the dominant person) and a victim (the submissive person) can be identified.

Lastly, we can also talk about people who have developed dependent personalities, due to a fusion of certain characteristics of those who typically tend to create dependent bonds. They tend to relate to others (friends, family, and partners) in a somewhat obsessive manner, which can lead to toxic relationships. That said, having a dependent personality type does not necessarily mean being in an emotionally dependent relationship. A person can have a dependent personality and, at the same time, be in a healthy relationship where both people's emotional needs are being met. This is especially true if the person with this personality type is also working on their personal development to help them understand where this pattern comes from and trying to become more emotionally "independent".

Needless to say, any of these four concepts entail emotional discomfort, but we also know that not everything starts out that badly. Let's look at the phases of a relationship and where these problems might start to arise, or in other words, where the life lessons we've been subjected to over our lives begin being reflected in our relationships.

♥ 2 ♥

THE STAGES OF LOVE

1. ATTRACTION

Imagine this. You've unexpectedly met someone. A friend of a friend, someone you've been thinking about for months, your high school crush, or someone you've just happened to meet on an app.

You really want to be with this person. You've got it bad. Every day, you imagine what it would be like to be with them, happily spending time together and having sex. Even if you've already been on several dates with this person, you keep fantasizing about them. Speaking to them on the phone puts a goofy smile on your face. It's as if you have fallen under their spell.

2. FALLING IN LOVE / INFATUATION / THE HONEYMOON PERIOD

This is the stage where all the myths we've been fed about romantic love and all the unwritten rules come into play.

After getting to know each other a bit more over the course of several dates and through long WhatsApp conversations lasting late into the night, you realize you feel deeply connected. You feel so in love you believe this person is the love of your life. Everything is beautiful and you don't see any red flags (or if you do, you don't attach much importance to them). How is it possible that you never even knew this person existed before? Where have they been all your life?

I'll let you in on something. This phase doesn't last forever, and nor should it. According to studies, it lasts for around three to four years (although I have known couples whose honeymoon stage only lasted a few months). I like to think of this as a phase of "temporary madness", as I believe our bodies are busy releasing a cocktail of substances, making us see and feel things which don't match reality. This hype can't last forever because, although it doesn't feel like it, the body is actually under stress. (Let's call it eustress, the positive form of stress, the one that makes you feel butterflies in your stomach and doesn't make you want to rip the heart out of your chest). Later on, I will explain how this works at a biochemical level.

However, I'm telling you this because, even though many people seem determined to make this phase of their relationship last forever, that's just not possible. If we all fell head over heels in love forever, the world would descend into chaos, and probably, in time, we'd all become ill because falling in love means, for our bodies at least, being in a state of high alert and relative chaos. This is why Mother Nature (in her wisdom) gradually guides us towards a state of stability.

3. DISAPPOINTMENT OR DISENCHANTMENT

This is the point at which we take off the rose-tinted glasses and realize just how blind that buzz from the brain-substance-cocktail made us.

I had a friend who, without knowing about these stages, always declared that she was cursed in relationships. She called it the three-year curse. She defined it specifically as a moment of crisis, when a couple would have to decide whether or not to continue with the relationship. I really hope that she reads this book and can understand that none of her relationships were cursed, it was simply that the honeymoon stage was drawing to an end, and the disappointment phase was kicking in.

"Why doesn't this person want to sleep with me anymore?" "Doesn't he like me anymore?", you might keep asking yourself. It may be that your conversations no longer feel especially deep, you're staying over at each other's places less often, or perhaps you're spotting behaviors you dislike.

Time goes by, and the first hints of disappointment creep in when you compare the petty troubles that crop up in the relationship with the wider myths and "truths" you were fed about romantic love; myths which you had previously accepted at face value.

In any relationship, without yet knowing whether this one will be healthy or not, this is the point at which you start to see your partner's flaws, you start requesting changes, and your partner asks for some changes from you too. This is where the danger lies, because whether or not the couple succeeds in building a healthy relationship all depends on how they face up to these issues.

If conflicts, when they crop up, are handled in a practical and flexible manner, the relationship will start to grow in a healthy direction.

During this phase, the couple goes through the well-known "coupling stage", which consists of getting to know one another and "adapting" to each other. It refers to noticing aspects of the relationship which are less than ideal, putting these to the other person and requesting changes, and/or suggesting possible solutions that both parties feel comfortable with, and then working towards making these changes happen.

So yes, it's time to get to work. But remember relationships require effort, not sacrifice.

---

4. REAL LOVE / MATURE LOVE / STABLE RELATIONSHIP

This should be the relationship goal for all relationships. However, what's most surprising is that this phase, characterized by feelings of peace and stability, is seen by many people as the "boring" stage of the relationship. They may even perceive it as lacking in love, but nothing could be further from the truth. There is certainly love, but it is just being experienced differently. It can be said that at this stage we have moved beyond infatuation, to feeling real love, a much more sophisticated and complex emotion.

This is the phase which sees true and faithful commitment being built, and where the most profound and measured decisions are taken. The couple's relationship has become a source of mutual support where communication, conversation, and negotiation take pride of place.

This is just how it is.

"What a *hater* of love you are," some say to me. It's not that I'm a hater, it's just that my job is to understand the processes underlying relationships in order to make sense of why things unfold the way they do. Or why my patients feel what they feel or think what they think.

So, while it's true that I'm not a fan of crushes, just like many people on this planet, I do *love* love. And I believe that falling in love (infatuation) can't last forever but love itself can.

♥ 3 ♥

MYTHS ABOUT LOVE AND ROMANCE

I mentioned earlier that at the "falling in love" or "infatuation" stage, we seem to intuit the myths around love and romance via some sort of collective consciousness, heralding our own learning journey and experiences of coupled relationships.

Myths about romantic love are essentially oversimplifications of the reality of relationships, which have the ability to influence our behavior. They are the breeding ground and lifeblood of toxic and dependent relationships, as well as those which, while maintaining practical bonds, are destined to end in frustration, dissatisfaction, and failure.

If you have ever pinpointed such myths hiding behind your ideas of what it actually means to be in a relationship, rest assured that you're not the only one. Our society provides the perfect environment to be bombarded with false beliefs about love that, inevitably, feed back into our behavior. Somehow, we have internalized the idea, both actively and passively, that these myths should become the blueprints for our relationships.

There are so many irrational beliefs about love and what being in a relationship should look like. You will already be familiar with, and easily able to identify, some of them, but there will be others that would surprise you. Myths about love and romance seem to have a subconscious hold on people. Therefore, as you read on, some of what follows and my reasoning may look like I'm stating the obvious, however these latent beliefs can remain, lurking, exerting a strong influence on the ideas you may have developed around love and relationships in general.

1. SEX WILL ALWAYS BE PASSIONATE, AND IF IT'S NOT, IT MEANS THE RELATIONSHIP IS OVER

We've all seen it before. Passion between two people has a tendency to wane over time. The reason is simple and can be summed up in just one word: overfamiliarity. Remember that the body cannot remain eternally in the "infatuation" stage.

People become accustomed to the things they often see and do, and this is no different when applied to our love lives.

The key to avoid falling into a routine is to keep things innovative in the bedroom. Keep pursuing novel experiences to reignite the spark which might otherwise, over time, sputter out. Sometimes going to therapy can be a good solution to this, since in addition to gaining psychosexual and relationship education, you can also learn exercises to do by yourself and as a couple, which can help to fan the flames of desire.

2. IF MY PARTNER LOVED ME, HE'D ACCEPT ME JUST AS I AM, AND WOULDN'T ASK ME TO CHANGE AT ALL

When we first meet someone and fall in love, we see them as perfect. We idealize them, without keeping in mind that we are all just people at the end of the day, and people are riddled with imperfections. But time is what's required in order for couples to face everyday life and its many challenges together.

We all have different perspectives, different opinions, and different reactions to things, mainly influenced by our own personal experiences. So, we must always bear in mind that we are all fundamentally different from one another, (and this is also of course what makes us special).

You may have hundreds of things in common with your partner, but that doesn't mean that you will always be one hundred percent on the same page about everything. It's around these points of difference that negotiation must take place to reach agreements which you both feel comfortable with. It's important to note that this is not about changing the person, this is about changing how the person behaves within the relationship. I'm emphasizing this latter point because a typical phrase that I often hear from many of the couples I see in my practice is "this is just the way I am. If you like it, fine, and if you don't, at least you know what to expect."

This phrase is completely out of place within the context of a relationship. When you're in the coupling stage it is entirely necessary to change any dysfunctional behaviors affecting how the relationship works, but, clearly, changing behaviors is not the same as changing a particular way of being. There are those who don't understand this because they can't separate the person they are from the things that they do.

If, by chance, your partner is one of those who can't tell one from the other, I would recommend explaining to them that in psychology, we "operationalize symptoms", or in other words, we divide people's responses into four distinct categories:

- **Behavioral responses**: Actions, e.g. going to the gym, reading a book, talking with your partner, cleaning the house, cooking, etc.
- **Cognitive responses:** Thoughts, e.g. going round in circles fixating on problems, "what if things don't turn out the way I hope?".
- **Emotional responses:** Feelings, e.g. happiness, sadness, jealousy, anxiety, fear, etc.
- **Physiological responses**: What's happening inside your body; physical symptoms, e.g. headache, insomnia, feeling a sense of pressure in your chest, etc.

And nothing, absolutely nothing about these responses, defines the person who is having them. This is basically because our responses are as changeable as the wind. Today they can be one thing and tomorrow they can be something else. But the person themselves, their values, their essence, and the core of their being, all remain constant. We may make mistakes in our responses to things, but not when it comes down to who we actually are as a person.

3. MY PARTNER SHOULD KNOW WHAT I THINK, FEEL, AND NEED BECAUSE THEY KNOW ME

Loving someone does not come with any particular psychic powers to determine what they need. Communication is a fundamental aspect of being in a couple. Talking about thoughts, feelings, and needs is essential for the other person to be able to act on them.

It's a mistake to expect the other person in a relationship to anticipate these things, because it is possible to get it wrong, and when they do, it's probably going to cause a certain amount of frustration to both sides: both the one who guessed wrongly because they didn't know any better, and also to the one who has not felt understood.

There is a famous quote doing the rounds on the Internet (supposedly by Frida Kahlo) that I shall take it upon myself to correct. It went something like this:

IF I HAVE TO ASK YOU FOR IT,
I NO LONGER WANT IT.

I will ask you for it because you cannot read my mind and communication is the only tool I can use to express my requests.

4. IF MY PARTNER LOVES ME, THEY WILL NEVER BE ANGRY WITH ME

As people, we don't actively choose when we get angry, nor indeed when we feel any other emotion, but we can certainly learn to manage our emotions, handle our anger, and communicate with others assertively.

In any relationship it's necessary and normal to get angry and experience conflicts, though not fights. In my opinion, those are two completely different things. Fights are conflicts which have gotten out of hand. But the conflicts themselves, however, are actually opportunities to communicate, express our opinions, listen to those of our partner and reach agreements (if that's what the situation dictates). Therefore, it is not bad to clash about something or with someone, it is only a problem if you don't know how to handle it.

I wrote about communication in my book *Ama tu sexo* [*Love Your Sex*], where you'll find numerous tools and techniques to practice being assertive, with step-by-step step instructions. For those who have not read it, there are three types of communication: passive, aggressive, and assertive. In order to resolve conflicts, as I said, I recommend using an assertive style. Let's examine an example of each to gain an understanding of what resolving conflicts would look like using each of these distinct communication styles.

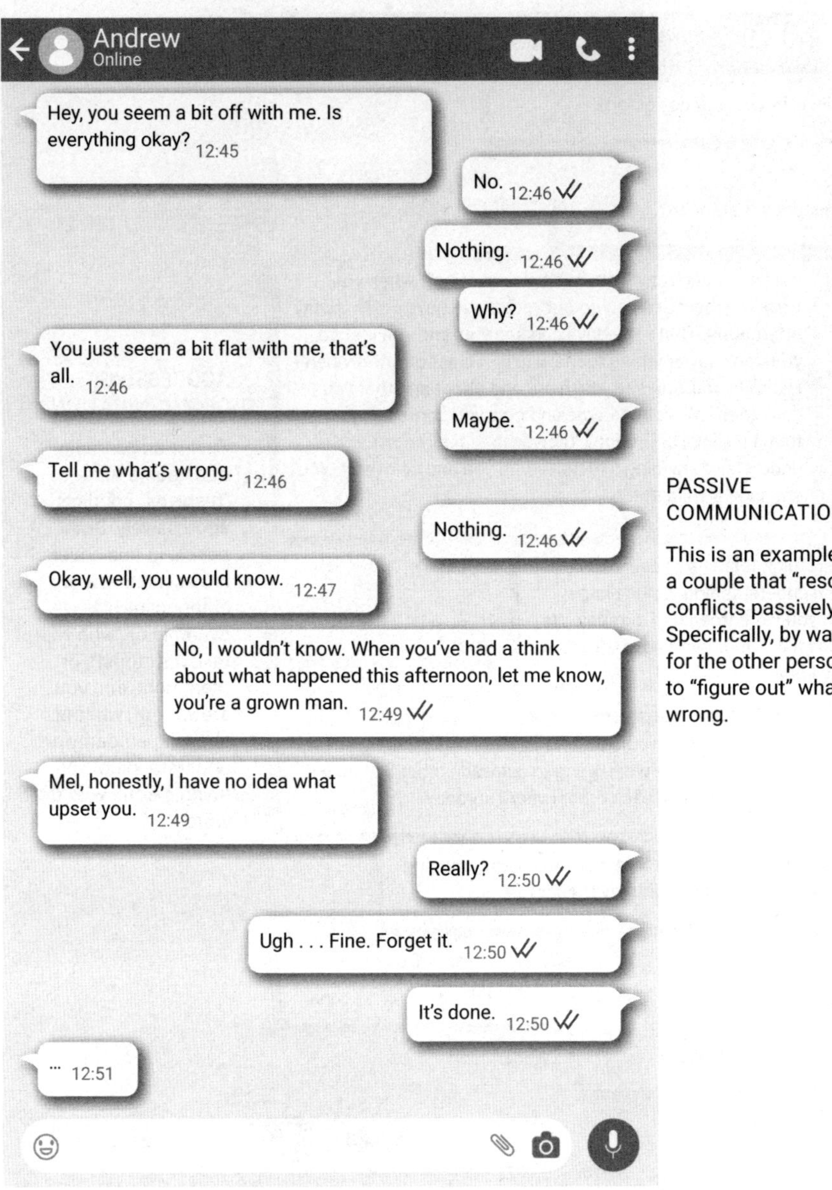

PASSIVE COMMUNICATION

This is an example of a couple that "resolves" conflicts passively. Specifically, by waiting for the other person to "figure out" what's wrong.

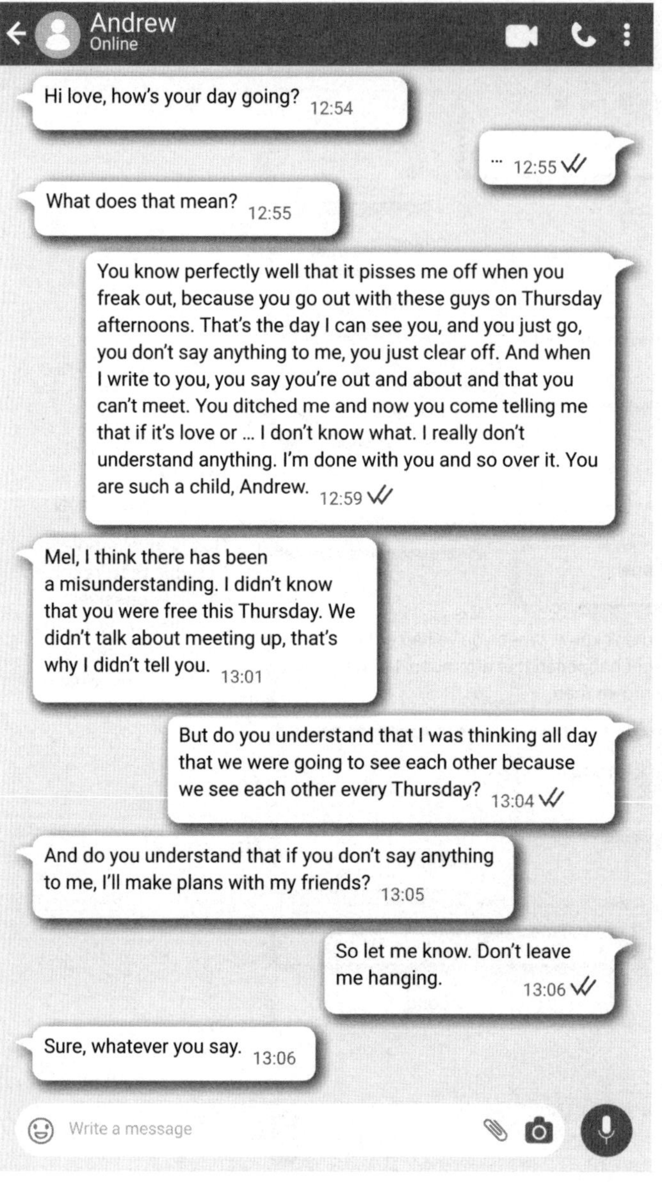

AGGRESSIVE COMMUNICATION

This is an example of a couple that "resolves" conflicts aggressively. Both people in this couple are escalating and entering into the dynamic of "who will take it furthest", or "I am right, and you are wrong", without showing empathy or understanding, nor being careful with their words.

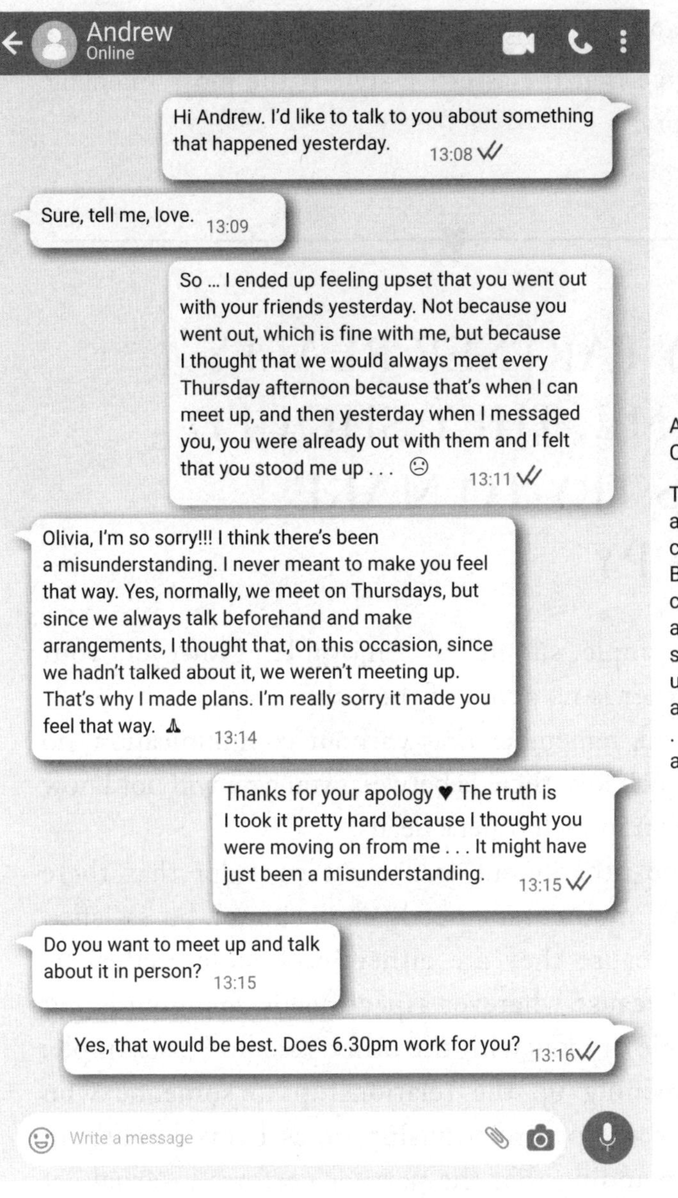

ASSERTIVE COMMUNICATION

This is an example of a couple that resolves conflicts assertively. Both members of the couple are paying attention to their tone, showing empathy and understanding, to unite against the problem . . . In this case, a misunderstanding.

The WhatsApp screenshots speak for themselves. I think we can all agree that the assertive style is the most amenable and conciliatory.

---

5. IF MY PARTNER REALLY LOVES ME, THEY SHOULD ALWAYS TRY TO MAKE ME HAPPY

Being in a couple should be enjoyable. However, your romantic partner is no genie of the lamp.

On one hand, remember that without communication, no matter how much love there is between you, you will not know what is going on in each other's heads.

And, on the other hand, you must consider that there are sometimes momentary needs that cannot be satisfied as we wish because they are either impossible, materially speaking, or because whatever aspect needs changing is not actually feasible or okay with the other person. For example: suggesting opening up the relationship to someone who does not want an open relationship or, as I saw recently in my clinic, demanding that the partner perform a sexual act that they're very averse to (even if it's considered something quite normal in practice).

6. IF WE ARE IN LOVE, WE WILL NEVER FALL OUT

We all have emotions and feelings and, as such, we have the right to feel upset, not only with our partner, but also about anything that feels inappropriate to us.

If your partner does something that bothers you or that is not to your liking, you should let them know so that they are aware of your discomfort, and can take it into consideration in future, leading to a change in their behavior. And vice versa, it takes two to tango. As I mentioned in the fourth myth, arguing is not a bad thing, nor does it indicate that the relationship is going downhill, it actually helps us to negotiate and clarify matters. It's only a bad thing if arguments get out of hand, if what's being said is met with an aggressive attitude, if they're constant, if one partner imposes their will on the other, or if the issues which were meant to be resolved keep being repeated or thrown in your face.

7. BEING IN LOVE MEANS WANTING TO BE TOGETHER ALL THE TIME

Spending 24 hours a day together without giving the other person some breathing space is not healthy.

It's lovely to want to be with your partner and see them all the time, but spending too much time together can lead to petty arguments over little things that don't really matter. That's exactly what happened to many couples after the Covid-19 lockdowns in 2020.

Missing each other and then meeting up again (not necessarily after a long time) is also lovely. Plus, we all have responsibilities to attend to. If your partner doesn't want to spend every minute of the day with you, that doesn't mean they don't love you; it means that, in addition to loving you, they also fulfil their responsibilities towards their work, their family, and their friends. These are also all-important parts of a person's life.

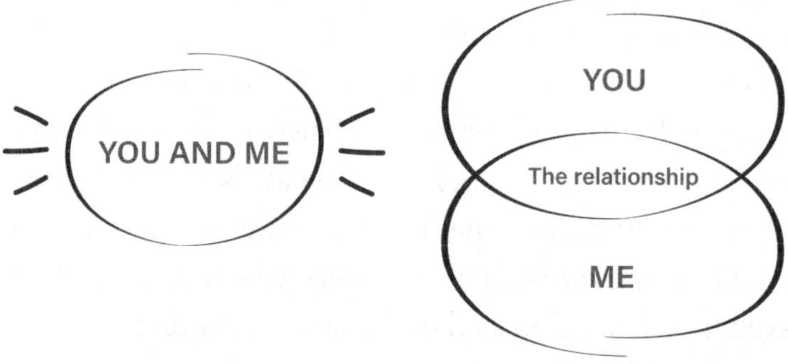

I have noticed that myths evolve and give way to new ones. I have also noticed that among younger people individualistic attitudes to relationships are becoming normalized. "We are boyfriend/girlfriend, but I keep my life separate: I hang out with my friends every weekend, I play sports, I study or work, I do my hobbies, and when I've got free time, I hang out with my partner." In other words, this is a full-blown "I have a partner, but only for when I have time to spare" situation. Is a relationship just a complement to a person's life? It's fine to do all this, but if you have a partner, you do also have to make time for them. If this is your situation, remember that you must accept that you have a responsibility to show affection to your partner. I will expand on this topic later.

8. WE WILL ALWAYS SHARE THE SAME INTERESTS, GOALS, AND VALUES

Throughout the course of our lives, we all go through a variety of situations which demand that we learn and grow from the experience. They influence all of us, and no, these experiences cannot be avoided. People change and relationships evolve. To deny this would be like saying that water is always liquid, when we know that's not true; it can be ice, liquid, or vapor, depending on the context.

9. WE SHOULD ALWAYS AGREE WITH EACH OTHER ON IMPORTANT ISSUES

Now here we have two issues. On the one hand, yes, it is convenient to have shared values and similar life goals, if we want the relationship to last. But on the other hand, not everyone considers the same things to be important. So, it's crucial to listen to your partner, validate their opinions and emotions, and accept them for who they are.

And afterwards, if necessary, you can come to some agreements.

10. IF I'M ATTRACTED TO ANOTHER PERSON, IT MEANS OUR LOVE IS OVER

Nothing could be further from the truth. Placing importance on a person's physique, real or fictitious, or feeling attracted to them is not synonymous with no longer feeling attracted to your partner, or with infidelity. But here lies a dilemma, because there are people who, in the 21st century, still confuse attraction, a physiological process, with infidelity, a social construct, or the absence of love, a complex emotion.

Actually, it is normal to feel love for one person and attraction to another because love and attraction are processed in different parts of the brain.

A while ago I talked about this on my Instagram profile (@maria_esclapez) and my followers sent me some questions about it. Here's what I told them.

When a person feels attraction, he or she usually starts having sexual fantasies. That is, they imagine themselves having sexual encounters with the person they are attracted to.

These fantasies are nothing more than cognitive phenomena (remember the way that we psychologists categorize the four responses), which means that we don't have to put them out of our minds if we don't want to, and they have nothing at all to do with our behavior. Be mindful, because we're not obliged to share them with our partner either. In our minds we are free.

I was asked about whether there is a way to deal with being attracted to one person while being in love with another, without actually committing infidelity, and yes, there certainly is. You can channel this desire into masturbation or having sex with your partner. This is where all hell breaks loose, because, sure, masturbating while thinking about someone else, okay, but how can I avoid feeling bad about it if I know that my partner is thinking about someone else while we're having a sexual encounter? But this is what I'd ask: how could you ever know what the other person is thinking? The only way, as we have seen, would be for your partner to tell you, but why should he or she have to? If we were compelled to say everything we think out loud, wouldn't that remove our freedom of thought? Wouldn't this fall under the umbrella of being "too honest", by deliberately hurting your partner with unimportant information, in this case? (I will explore this idea in more detail later.)

My followers also raised the possibility of feeling guilty about thinking of someone else while they were with their partner in an intimate situation. But you know what? Thoughts are only that, just thoughts. Your head doesn't know if what it's thinking is good or bad, the moral burdens or the connotations of such thoughts are placed there by you. And knowing this, my dear reader, is to move up a step on the scale of sexual intelligence.

I'll reiterate: having sexual fantasies has nothing to do with making them come true. Moreover, there are people who are happy fantasizing in their heads, and in private, but just by thinking about making those fantasies come true, they get cold feet. It bursts their bubble, (which doesn't mean that they don't still think about them). So, you can see that there is a big difference between what people think and what they actually do.

Some also believe that fantasizing about someone who you know makes you more likely to be unfaithful than if you were to, for instance, fantasize about a celebrity. And yes, this might possibly be true if we were all automatons, but that is not the case. However, when it does happen, one explanation (among others), is that the person lost self-control in the moment.

Obviously, satisfying your lust with the object of your desire is not a good idea, (at least within a closed relationship, where exclusivity is assumed). So, for this reason, I wouldn't include it on the list of possibilities.

11. PRINCE CHARMING EXISTS

Here's a snippet from an article that I wrote a while ago on the Badoo website, a well-known global dating app, in which I think I've perfectly captured the implications of having this myth swirling around in our heads:

> Soulmates, Prince Charming ... Who hasn't heard of these myths before? Nowadays, I can't stand them. But there was once a time when I believed them, and they were very firmly held beliefs at

that, because nobody ever taught me otherwise. No one ever said that there was no Prince Charming somewhere out there on the horizon, waiting to one day find me and rescue me from my life and all my own mistakes. Nobody ever said that life isn't like it is in the films, with a meet-cute where girl meets boy, they say all the right things, and magically, after a series of misadventures, she realizes that he is the love of her life, and that wonderfully, her feelings are reciprocated. No one ever questioned or deconstructed the idea of romantic love. On the contrary, it permeated all the films, series, and books. It was held up as the ideal of a perfect relationship. And what an ideal; woe betide the person who tried to make it a reality, emotional dependence would surely come knocking at their door. At least, that's what happened to me.

Influenced by all the lies I was told growing up, I entered the world of relationships. I wanted to be the perfect person, who finds their perfect person, and for everything to turn out perfectly. High expectations? Not at all, it was what I saw all around me, it was the norm. Pressure? A little, truth be told. Every date was THE DATE. You catch my drift. I felt that there was no room for failure [. . .], that I had to find that unique and wonderful person, that non-existent Prince Charming who would be able to guess my thoughts and do what I was always hoping for him. Of course, everything always turned out badly.

So, Prince Charming, also known as "the perfect person", of any sex or gender, doesn't exist. We all have our good qualities and our faults.

And, I am sorry to say, no one is coming to save you from your emotional discomfort, just like no one came to save me, nor anyone else on the planet, ever, for that matter.

12. WE ALL NEED TO FIND OUR SOULMATE; IF WE DON'T, OUR LIVES ARE UNFULFILLED

Sharing life with someone else is lovely and can be a very enriching experience, however this decision should never be taken out of a sense of "need". Human beings are already complete, just as we are.

13. IF THEY FEEL JEALOUS IT'S BECAUSE THEY LOVE ME OR CARE ABOUT ME

Although I'll expand upon this in another chapter, I will say right now that jealousy is not love, it's a reflection of fears and insecurities.

A person may value someone very highly, love and care about them, but also succumb to jealousy. However, such jealousy is not an indication of the love they profess.

14. LOVE IS ALL YOU NEED

Love is necessary in a relationship, but it's insufficient on its own. Other tools are necessary to be able to maintain a relationship over time: communication skills, empathy, problem solving, the ability to manage emotions, etc.

Imagine a relationship where the couple lacks respect for each other, where everything is a fight, where they don't communicate or even spend much time together. The couple might swear that there is love, but the love they feel is insufficient for the relationship to function properly.

15. OPPOSITES ATTRACT

Well, it certainly should be said that we are people, not magnets, but, even so, I would say that this myth is partly true and partly false.

A priori, the idea of being with someone very different to ourselves, can work out well because they can appear to "complement" us, so yes, we do tend to be attracted to those whom we imagine have the personal characteristics that we ourselves lack, as a strategy to complement ourselves and balance things out. For example: "Because I feel that I lack self-confidence, I look to people who seem very confident to support me." But, ha, this is a trap.

Later on, this will show up as an imbalance of roles, characterized by dominance (the confident person) and submission (the insecure person). And, in the long run, if these differences persist, the relationship may begin to cause suffering.

On the other hand, it's true that differences in our likes and dislikes exist, but the majority of toxic relationships are not toxic because one person likes pink and the other likes green, they're toxic because the people in them are polar opposites in the way that they relate to others, on the most intimate level, and in their ways of handling the most emotionally charged aspects of their relationship.

"And so the lion fell in love with the lamb ...", wrote Stephenie Meyer in her book *Twilight (2005).*

I used to believe in all this. Now, I am equal parts mortified and ashamed to admit that at 16 years old, reading that book, I was busy imagining what she would be like as a "lamb" and how nice being in a hypothetical relationship with a "lion" by my side would be.

---

16. LOVE IS FOREVER

There is no definitive guarantee whatsoever that a relationship will last forever. Not even a ring or a wedding can assure this. Sometimes relationships end and sometimes they keep going. Everything depends on how the relationship is managed. Having confidence in the relationship lasting is practically a leap of faith. If we focus too heavily on procuring "demonstrations" of love, as a way to reassure ourselves that it will last forever, we end up not only expending our energies in vain, but we can also find ourselves entering a vicious circle which is very hard to break.

WE CAN DRAW PARALLELS WITH PLANTS

Some plants can last forever while others perish. It all depends on how carefully we tend to them each and every day. If we look after our plants diligently each day, pamper them, pay proper attention to any dangers on the horizon (bad weather, infestations etc.), and solve those problems as they crop up, it's more likely that our plants will survive much longer. If, on the other hand, we only water them from time to time, no matter how much we may want our plants to live a long and healthy life, they are more likely to wilt sooner. Even if we dearly wish they would last forever. Sometimes, even if we take great care of them, our plants may still die for reasons beyond our control. Nothing guarantees success, but pouring more of the right kind of care and attention into a plant increases the probability that it will flourish for much longer.

17. LOVE IS WHEN "TWO BECOME ONE"

Love simply cannot be some sort of two-for-one deal (two people morphing into one, in some sort of utopian, inclusive fusion), as each person has their own identity, their own thoughts, emotions, behaviors, and ways of seeing things. We cannot "meld into" the other person, and nor should we, no matter how much we adore them. We might love them to the ends of the earth, but mimicking them in every way can be risky, in that we can end up losing our own sense of identity and what makes us unique ourselves. For this reason, the model we should really be using to help define our couple relationships is that of "interdependence".

Types of romantic relationships:

♥ SUBSUMED

ONE PERSON IN THE COUPLE IS DEPENDENT ON THE OTHER. THERE IS NO SPACE FOR INDEPENDENCE.

♥ UTOPIAN FUSION

TYPICAL OF FALLING IN LOVE: EVERYTHING IS SHARED, THERE IS NO SPACE FOR INDEPENDENCE.

♥ INTERDEPENDENT

THINGS ARE SHARED, BUT EACH PERSON HAS SPACE TO BE THEMSELVES.

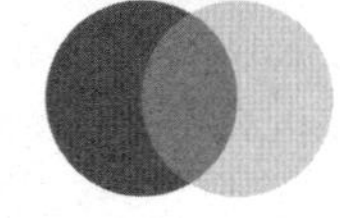

♥ TOTAL SEPARATION

NOTHING IS SHARED.

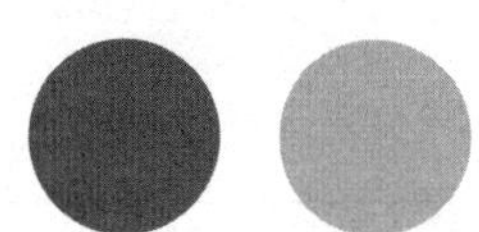

Back in my first relationship, I idealized my partner so much that I practically morphed into him! I'm ashamed to admit it now, because at the time I staunchly insisted that that's how I had always been. But that just wasn't true. I became more like him than myself. I listened to his music, copied his style in clothing, and even convinced myself that we thought alike, spouting the kind of things that he used to say. This was all done unconsciously, but I think it was my brain's way of desperately trying to avoid another abandonment, because before this all happened, I had already gone through the trauma of breaking up and getting back together with him, without explanation. I figured, if I acted and spoke the same way as he did, then I would gain his approval and create a stronger bond, and consequently he would never leave me. (Spoiler alert, it didn't work. He left me again because he said that I had changed. He wasn't wrong.) What's interesting about this is just how far you can manage to convince yourself to believe it. That's the power of the mind and the trouble with having low self-esteem, honey. Nowadays, since I like to make fun of my sob stories, it makes me laugh to think about how much I used to wish I looked like, I don't know, Beyoncé or something.

♥

18. FRICTION CREATES HEAT

This idea that arguments go hand-in-hand with desire is often suggested when there is apparently some sort of "unresolved sexual tension" between two people. And there are those who defend it too, saying that they don't know how to get close to the person they like in any other way.

Steamy make-up sessions after a fight also add fuel to the fire. But in truth, this is all a bit of an urban myth. In the next few chapters, we'll dive into why these sorts of dramas and explosive reconciliations happen. And I'll tell you now, it has nothing to do with this myth.

If you're fighting with someone, it's not because you desire them, it's because you're fighting. End of story.

19. LOVE IS THE MOST IMPORTANT THING AND REQUIRES YOU TO GIVE IT EVERYTHING YOU'VE GOT

Love is important.

Romantic relationships are important.

But the idea of "giving oneself totally" is related to the philosophy of "sacrifice" and tireless giving, even if you get nothing in return, which just doesn't work.

It goes without saying that codependent people cling tightly to this myth to justify their behavior and their extreme preoccupation with their partner.

In relationships between couples, it is necessary to create a balance of give-and-take. That doesn't mean measuring every little thing, but you do need to notice whether or not effort seems mutual and that signs of affection, whatever they may be, are reciprocal. Sometimes one person in the couple will be giving more than the other, and vice versa, but the important thing is that there should always be a balance over time.

20. ONCE I AM IN A RELATIONSHIP, I "BELONG" TO MY PARTNER

"You're mine, only mine" (*Fifty Shades of Grey*, E.L. James), Christian Grey said to Anastasia Steele.

"Eres Mia (You are mine)," sang Alejandro Sanz.

"Ever thine, ever mine, ever ours," (*Sex and the City: The Movie*) repeated Carrie Bradshaw and Mr. Big, inspired by Beethoven's letters to his beloved.

"You're mine" (*Twilight*, Stephenie Meyer), said Edward Cullen to Bella Swan.

Is it any coincidence that when we think of these situations, most of the time it's a man saying this to a woman? I'll leave it there.

But never forget: you belong to yourself. Being in a couple is not about possession, it's about sharing.

By now, you must have realized that true love is not found, it is built. And that falling in love is easy, but learning how to love is not.

Oh, honey, they sold it to us as love, and we believed it! Let's see an example of how this myth plays out in everyday life.

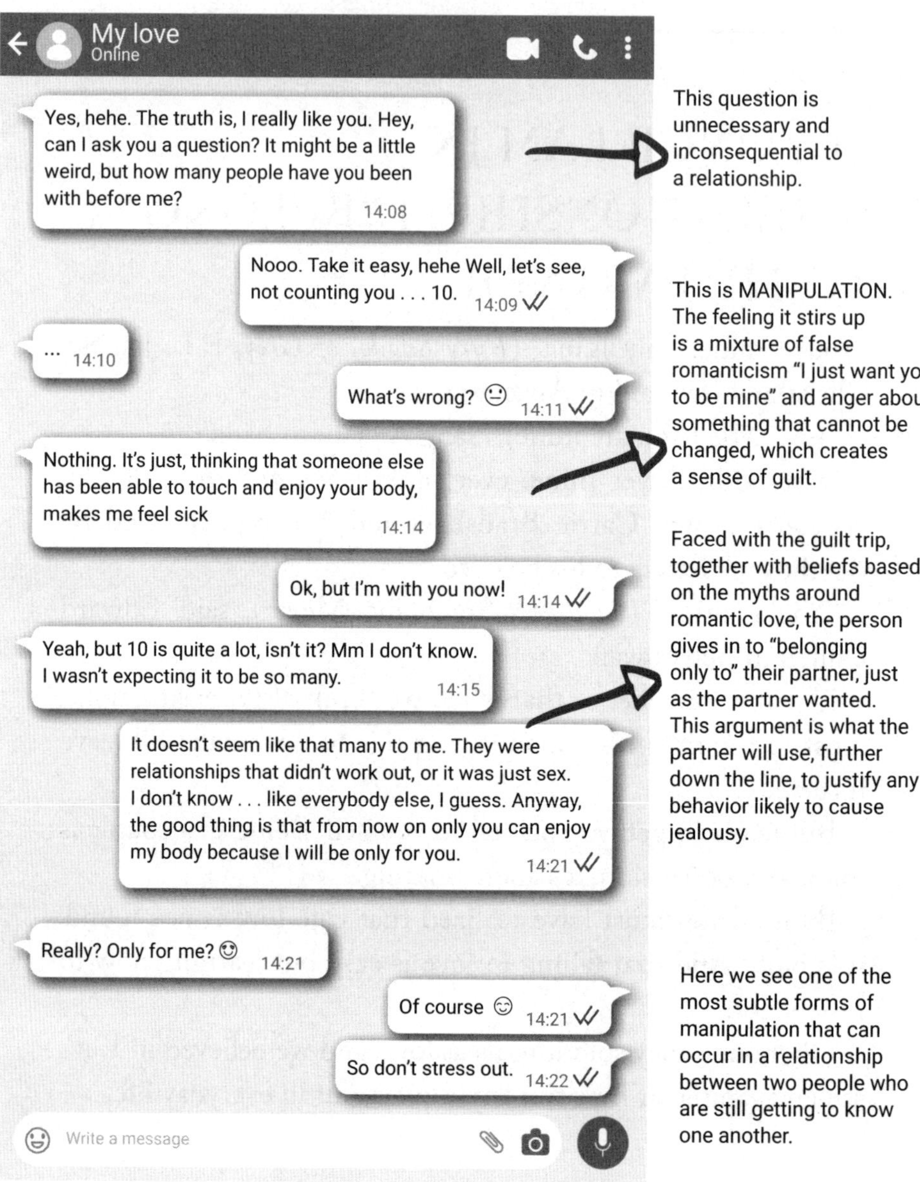

This question is unnecessary and inconsequential to a relationship.

This is MANIPULATION. The feeling it stirs up is a mixture of false romanticism "I just want you to be mine" and anger about something that cannot be changed, which creates a sense of guilt.

Faced with the guilt trip, together with beliefs based on the myths around romantic love, the person gives in to "belonging only to" their partner, just as the partner wanted. This argument is what the partner will use, further down the line, to justify any behavior likely to cause jealousy.

Here we see one of the most subtle forms of manipulation that can occur in a relationship between two people who are still getting to know one another.

♥ 4 ♥

HOW TO IDENTIFY EMOTIONAL DEPENDENCE

We have just walked through an important part of the context to everything that follows.

Knowing how to identify whether or not you are in an emotionally dependent relationship is fundamental to determining the kind of relationship you are in.

Are you ready? Breathe, some of the things you read next may leave you feeling a bit stirred up.

♥

GETTING THE FEELING THAT SOMETHING ISN'T RIGHT

This is the one thing you can always count on about dependent relationships. And, when you're experiencing it from the inside, you have an inexplicable sensation of constant unease. That, honey, is anxiety.

♥

LACK OF BALANCE AND SENSE OF SACRIFICE

This fact originates from one of the myths about romantic love that I talked about before: "Love is about giving without receiving anything in return."

This reminds me of the case of Clara, a 35-year-old woman married to Enrique, 38. They had a child together. I remember when I saw them walk into my office together. She was the only one who spoke, while Enrique behaved as if it was nothing to do with him. My impression, after an hour and a half long session, was that the only one who seemed interested in saving this relationship was Clara, and that she was probably a codependent woman. He, despite having gambling problems, never returned to therapy, but she continued to see me weekly for a whole year.

"It's such hard work for me to maintain this relationship, María. I'm exhausted. I have lost a lot of weight, and I feel like I just can't take it anymore. I have tried to talk to Enrique a thousand times, but I just don't know what else to do."

Clara is one of those people who it is impossible not to like. She is a responsible, attentive, caring woman, and an absolute supermom! She could handle everything, her son, her job, her home, and her relationship. But everyone has their limit.

"Last week we had a very serious conversation," she told me on another occasion. "We sat on the sofa while the child slept, and I made it crystal clear to him that I can't take it anymore. He seems to have got his act together for now, but I'm afraid that in the next few days everything will slide back to normal. I feel like I'm the only one pulling in the right direction."

And it was true, and Enrique did just carry on as normal. It was interesting to me that Clara's concept of normality was that her husband did not fully participate in the relationship. And that we can get used to everything, even things which make us suffer.

Clara and Enrique are still together, but the progress she made in therapy was incredible. She took it very seriously, realized her situation and stopped being one of those "women who love too much."

Now let's look at the case of Diego, a 24-year-old man whose toxic and dependent relationship can help illustrate my next points.

THE PARTNER IS THE TOP PRIORITY

Diego was a great guy. Hard-working, sporty, intelligent, and good-looking. He came to my clinic because he was worried about his relationship. He was with a girl of the same age, Olaya, that he had met through one of his friends. He said he was very happy with her, in general, but that sometimes there were situations which didn't leave him feeling very good.

We started talking and Diego admitted to me that, for him, Olaya came above all else. He gave me a few examples:

He told me that on weekends, before making any plans with his friends, he always asked her first whether she would like to do anything in particular. She, however, didn't say anything like that to him most of the time. She directly went out with her friends, and this led Diego to feel abandoned. Here, Diego was doing well, showing that he cared about his relationship and that he was considerate of Olaya as a part of his life, both when making plans as a couple and individually. Olaya, however, seemed to be miles away, completely distracted and distanced from the relationship.

He also told me that, usually, he would suggest plans, and she would reject them, but when she proposed a plan, he would drop whatever he was doing to go with her. Once, Diego was with his friends when Olaya texted him to say that she wanted to meet up right then and there. He quickly made up an excuse to leave his friends and went to meet her.

This no longer sounded to me like healthy prioritization, whereby the partner is given their rightful place in a person's life, and it was starting to sound more like she was an absolute priority, one of the characteristics of dependency in relationships.

On another occasion, Diego was studying for an exam that he was due to sit the next day. Olaya called him to say that she was feeling down, and he then spent the rest of the day more concerned about her than studying, leading him to fail his test.

I recalled an episode when, two weeks prior, Diego had undergone surgery that had left him with an abdominal scar and stitches, and she had insisted on going to the fair that weekend. Instead of staying home and resting, Diego made the effort to go with her to the fair, and he ended up bursting one of his stitches and had to return to hospital.

In these three occasions, Olaya was clearly Diego's first priority, however Diego is not top priority for Olaya. Broadly speaking, this may appear as something circumstantial or merely anecdotal. The solution seemed simple: talk to Olaya so that she could understand what was going on, and train Diego to set boundaries, learning to cultivate his self-esteem so that he could put himself as the priority, (always within the bounds of common sense, and while giving due consideration to Olaya in his day-to-day life). So far, there was nothing particularly worrying about the relationship itself, I usually note any dubious characteristics of the relationship in order to confirm my hypotheses. The problem revealed itself over subsequent sessions, in which things happened that, together with these anecdotes, made it start to look like a toxic and dependent relationship.

One day Diego came in crying, inconsolable.

"What's happened?" I asked, shocked.

"Olaya has left me. She said that she doesn't feel the same way about me anymore, and she thinks I can't make her happy."

As if Olaya's happiness depended on Diego. What a way to think about love! Olaya's attitude was starting to show. And this was something we could work with.

Diego told me everything in detail and we started working on how to tackle it in that very session.

THE RELATIONSHIP IS ON-AGAIN-OFF-AGAIN. "NOT TOGETHER, BUT NOT REALLY APART"

Two weeks later I had another session with him.

"Diego, you're looking very happy, how have you been this fortnight?" I asked, smiling.

"Great, María, I've got back together with Olaya."

My face fell. It's not that I wasn't happy that Diego was back with Olaya, it's just that my suspicions were beginning to be confirmed. And, indeed, I was not wrong. Weeks went by and it became an endless cycle of breakups and reconciliations.

♥

THE DANGER OF DRAMA

Those who know me know that I like to make jokes and laugh a lot in my sessions (only when appropriate, of course). Laughter helps to de-escalate any issues. So, every time Diego told me something that his partner had said or done to him, I would say: "Again with the drama?" to which Diego smiled and replied: "Yes, María, again. What a story I've got for you today." Being with Olaya was like living in a soap opera. The breakups were very dramatic, and the makeups were very passionate. Every WhatsApp conversation with her that Diego showed me seemed like a scene out of *Twilight*.

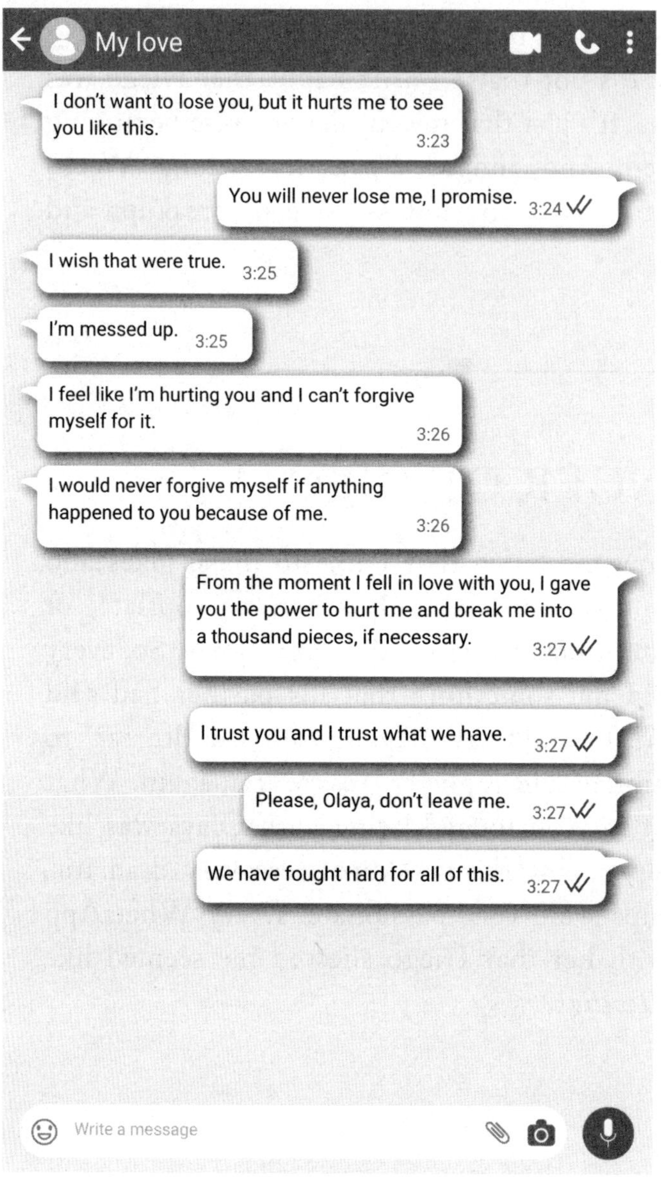

This conversation not only shows an inordinate level of intensity, but it is full of romantic clichés:

- "I'm putting myself in your hands."
- "I'm vulnerable."
- "I'm at your mercy."
- "My well-being depends on you."
- "I'm depending on you."
- "You, my partner, are responsible for my well-being."

Healthy relationships are egalitarian; there is no one above or below anyone else. The moment one person feels vulnerable in front of the other, that is when typical role stereotypes based on dominance and submission can arise.

Eventually he would come into the session saying "María, I'm bringing more drama," and we laughed because we already knew what was coming.

The bad thing about drama is that it's guaranteed to be an emotional rollercoaster.

Emotional rollercoasters are very typical of toxic relationships.

Feeling like you're on a rollercoaster is synonymous with having a good day followed by a bad day, it's a real mixed bag (like taking one step forward and one step back). Some people even admit that they don't know how to be in a relationship without having these ups and downs. What they probably don't know is that this perfectly epitomizes intermittent reinforcement, one of the most typical and dangerous phenomena associated with toxic and dependent relationships.

This concept, where a person gives you mixed signals, means that sometimes he or she behaves well towards you (reinforcement), but behaves badly towards you at others (punishment), and it is addictive. I'm telling you; it keeps you on the hook. Its effect is just like that of a drug. So much so that sometimes we even talk about it in terms of being, quite frankly, an addiction.

Intermittent reinforcement is one of the fastest patterns to be established, with some of the strongest conditioning. What's being reinforced is simply the way you relate to the other person. With intermittent reinforcement, we learn that being in a relationship is all about things going very well one day, (or for one stage), and very badly the next. We learn to always be alert to the possibility of something bad happening. We learn that love is full of drama and suffering, as well as passion and happiness. But in reality, this is not the case, although we do need to make an effort to move forward in a relationship, we do not need to be completely self-sacrificing. It shouldn't have to feel like an endurance test.

One of the reasons it is so hard to break free from dependent relationships is due to this addiction caused by all these emotional ups and downs. Just like when a person is addicted to a substance, in dependent relationships the people involved are "hooked" on this type of reinforcement, (mainly the codependent person, in this case Diego, who never knows when the next reinforcement in the form of a reconciliation is coming along, but he is hanging around for it anyway, because that's what's happened before).

The molecules responsible for these emotional ups and downs are dopamine, serotonin, phenylethylamine, endorphins, adrenaline, noradrenaline, and oxytocin. Depending on the levels of these substances, we will either feel the rush of a high or the low of a slump.

Oxytocin, also known as the love hormone, is released when we caress, kiss or hold our partner, when we have sex and, in short, when we feel loved. It's one of the substances responsible for the formation and strengthening of close bonds between people.

Serotonin is a neurotransmitter. When your levels decrease (which is what happens during infatuation), it causes you to constantly think about your crush. Once the relationship stabilizes and the couple's bonds are strong, serotonin levels rise again, creating a sense of emotional stability.

By the way, constantly turning over a thought or a matter in our heads is called *ruminating* (like cows when they eat, constantly chewing their food; we do the same, only with our thoughts).

Endorphins are substances that cause a lack of sensation of pain or suffering. That's why when you make up with your partner and everything is going well in the moment, you suddenly feel that whatever happened before (the drama) is unimportant. We could say that endorphins function as a kind of anesthetic.

Dopamine is the neurotransmitter of desire and pleasure, not only on a sexual level, but also for our sense of motivation in general. Dopamine is the predominant substance governing our brain's reward system, and in terms of relationships, it increases our motivation to be with our loved one.

When it comes to that feeling of being "hooked" on a special someone, dopamine and serotonin are the culprits, making us desire physical contact and want to spend all our time with them. To give you some idea of just how addictive these substances are, their levels are comparable to those of a person who is hooked on gambling or taking drugs.

Due to the effects of dopamine, being with the person you like can lead you to feel more energized, happy, motivated, with increased concentration and the feeling that nothing bad can happen.

That's what was happening to Diego. When everything was going well with Olaya, time seemed to fly. He was awarded "employee of the month", he signed up for courses and even felt that he didn't need to come to therapy anymore.

But, like a textbook case, this is also what happened to him when everything was going wrong with Olaya. During breakups, his dopamine levels dropped and Diego expressed his desperation to get back together with her, to get those feelings back (or, as he put it, "to go back to how it was before"), demonstrating that his brain really "missed" those high levels of dopamine.

Phenylethylamine which supports dopamine, is a substance which gives you a pleasant feeling, like floating on a cloud. Its effects last between three and four years (does this sound familiar?). That's the same length of time that the anthropologist Helen Fisher accords to the stages of falling in love.

Have you ever just been quietly chilling out at home when you receive a message from your crush and suddenly it feels like your heart's about to burst? That's partly down to dopamine, my friend! And partly down to noradrenaline.

Noradrenaline is another substance which induces euphoria and excitement (remember to think of these concepts broadly, not only in terms of sexuality), causing feelings of nervousness, blushing, nervous laughter, sweating, or feeling like your heart's about to burst out of your chest.

Adrenaline, which works together with noradrenaline, is released during periods of stress and anxiety, and, in this case, when falling in love, as counterintuitive as that may seem. The fact remains that falling in love is, in reality, an anomalous phase for the body, which is more accustomed to the stability of everyday life. Adrenaline causes a racing pulse and is responsible for that phenomenon where your mouth suddenly goes dry.

BUTTERFLIES IN YOUR STOMACH? THAT'S DOWN TO ADRENALINE.

Adrenaline increases peristalsis or, in other words, it gives you butterflies in your stomach. Peristalsis is how we describe the physical contractions of the digestive tract, which allow its contents to progress all the way down from the stomach to the anus. So, when you have butterflies in your tummy, what you're really experiencing is anxiety.

Levels of adrenaline and noradrenaline reduce whenever we are thwarted in love, which translates into passive behavior and a tremendous lack of energy.

All these substances, between the emotional highs and lows, are responsible for withdrawal symptoms, that sense of longing for a partner and for what you experienced together.

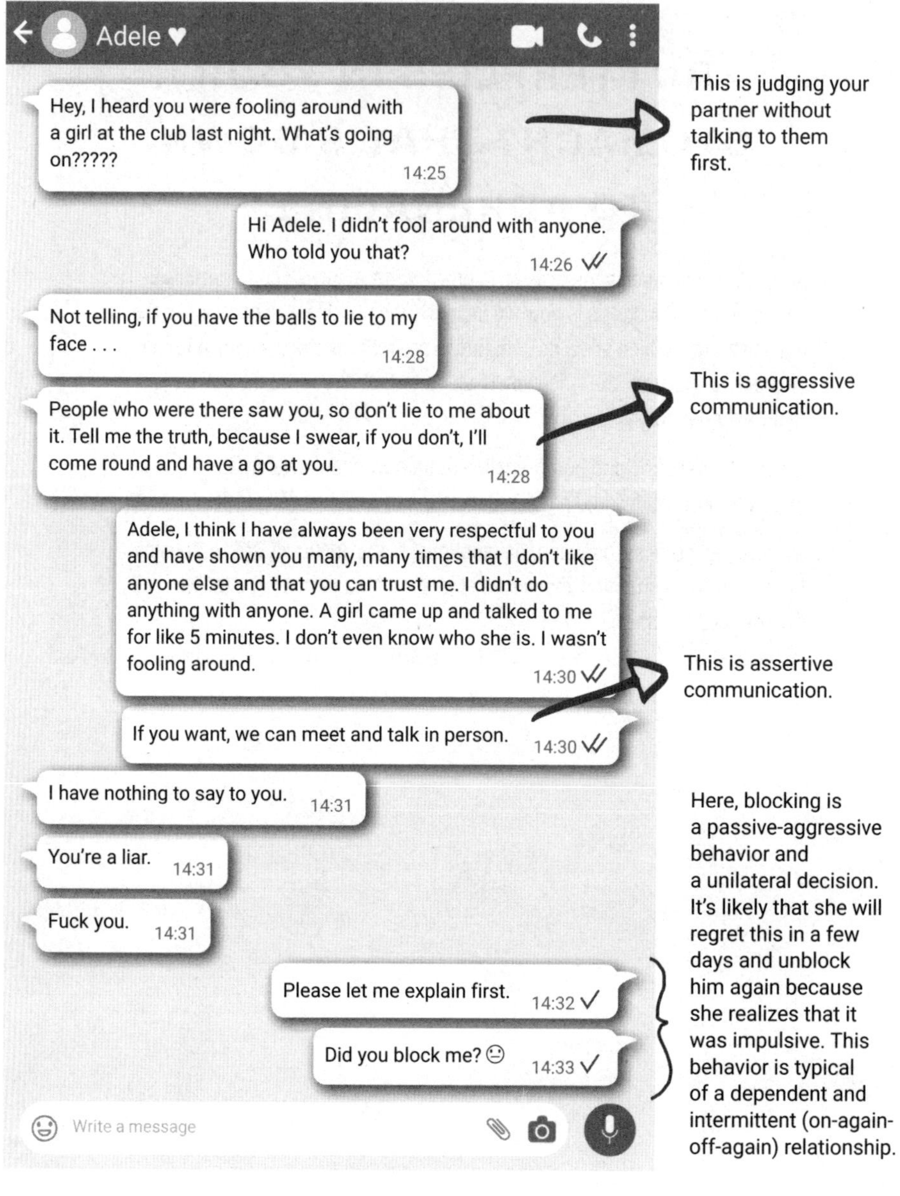
Adele ♥
Hey, I heard you were fooling around with a girl at the club last night. What's going on????? 14:25
Hi Adele. I didn't fool around with anyone. Who told you that? 14:26
Not telling, if you have the balls to lie to my face . . . 14:28
People who were there saw you, so don't lie to me about it. Tell me the truth, because I swear, if you don't, I'll come round and have a go at you. 14:28
Adele, I think I have always been very respectful to you and have shown you many, many times that I don't like anyone else and that you can trust me. I didn't do anything with anyone. A girl came up and talked to me for like 5 minutes. I don't even know who she is. I wasn't fooling around. 14:30
If you want, we can meet and talk in person. 14:30
I have nothing to say to you. 14:31
You're a liar. 14:31
Fuck you. 14:31
Please let me explain first. 14:32
Did you block me? ☹ 14:33
Write a message
This is judging your partner without talking to them first.
This is aggressive communication.
This is assertive communication.
Here, blocking is a passive-aggressive behavior and a unilateral decision. It's likely that she will regret this in a few days and unblock him again because she realizes that it was impulsive. This behavior is typical of a dependent and intermittent (on-again-off-again) relationship.

As we can see from this WhatsApp conversation, Adele's anger causes her to give in to the impulse to block her partner. This will lead her straight into withdrawal symptoms, where her amygdala, the part of the brain responsible for impulsive behavior, deactivates and gives way to all the other feelings typical of emotional lows caused by changes to the levels of all the relevant substances in the brain. In other words, when Adele's temper cools off, the anger will disappear, and she will start to regret her actions. What usually happens in these situations is that the impulsive person tends to initiate an approach to their partner, to apologize and hopefully try again.

THE RELATIONSHIP IS STUCK IN A CYCLE OF CONFLICT AND RECONCILIATION

The on-again off-again nature of toxic relationships is cyclical, and, throughout the whole process, three distinct phases can be identified:

Falling in love (infatuation) or the honeymoon phase:

As I explained in the previous chapter, this is the phase where you are so infatuated with your partner that you consider them to be the love of your life. You feel that your bond is special, magical, and better than any other relationship you've ever had before. All your past partners pale in comparison. The chemistry between you is very strong and you won't know if the relationship will work out unless you try. So, trusting in your love for each other, you take the leap. Fate finally has something so good in store for you that is better than even the best Hollywood rom-coms. Your days of suffering, when you thought you would never fall in love again, are long gone.

Tension:

What are known as "red flags" begin to show in the relationship, behaviors that, without really understanding why, start to become habitual.

You notice that just when you casually need to ask your partner for a favor, they are never available, they seem cold in the face of your hurt, and you are only their priority when they are interested in getting something from you.

In the next chapter we will discuss what "red flags" actually are in more depth, and I will provide examples so that you can identify whether there could be any in your relationships.

At first you don't pay them much attention; what you two have is special, and nothing and no one could ever come between you. You conclude that your problems are just the result of misunderstandings, or isolated incidents, and you use this to explain away all the times your partner has hurt you. Nevertheless, bit by bit you notice that things have started to change, and you witness certain behaviors which do not align with the person you thought you knew. This creates what we call cognitive dissonance, which, when applied to these circumstances, implies some kind of mismatch between two thoughts, or between a thought and an emotion, a behavior which conflicts with your beliefs. *Spoiler alert*: This cognitive phenomenon will continue throughout the rest of the relationship.

The relationship turns hostile before your very eyes, while all you want is for things to go back to being good between you, to return to the way things were before.

Explosion or aggression:

This phase starts when the relationship becomes unsustainable. Arguments begin, when all the things that have been hurting you during the tension phase get thrown in each other's faces. Verbal abuse, pride, and arrogant, combative attitudes appear alongside shouting, insults, and/or passive-aggressive behavior.

At that point the scales have fallen from your eyes, and you realize that it has all been a big mistake, you no longer want to continue being in the relationship, and you decide to end it.

You deserve to be happy, and no one can take that away from you. There are plenty more fish in the sea.

Days go by (sometimes only hours) and, in the quiet after the storm, one of the two comes forward again. Brokenhearted, just when you have lost hope in everything and everyone, and with a tremendous feeling of emptiness lying like a weight upon your chest, the person reappears. It feels like the storm has begun to die down.

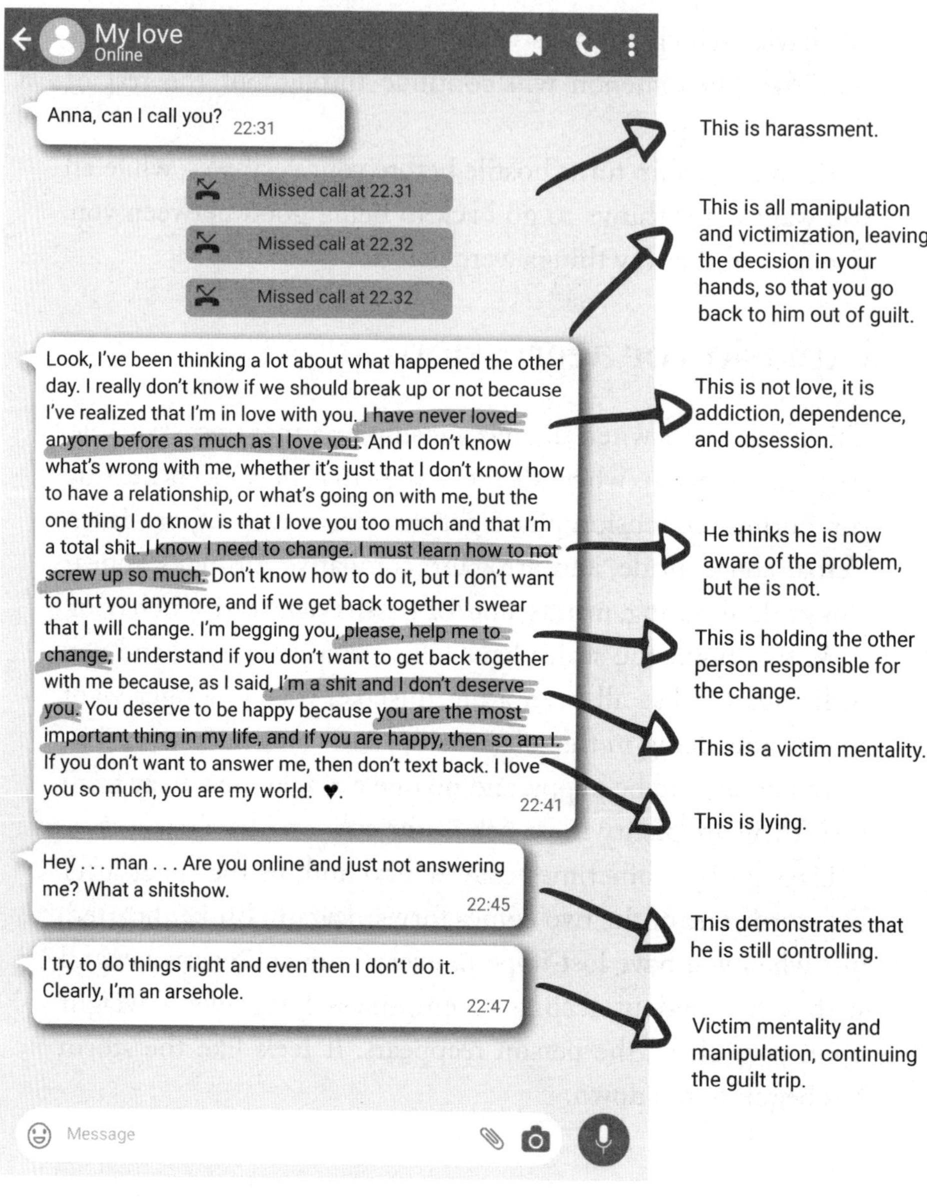
My love
Online
Anna, can I call you? 22:31
Missed call at 22.31
Missed call at 22.32
Missed call at 22.32
Look, I've been thinking a lot about what happened the other day. I really don't know if we should break up or not because I've realized that I'm in love with you. I have never loved anyone before as much as I love you. And I don't know what's wrong with me, whether it's just that I don't know how to have a relationship, or what's going on with me, but the one thing I do know is that I love you too much and that I'm a total shit. I know I need to change. I must learn how to not screw up so much. Don't know how to do it, but I don't want to hurt you anymore, and if we get back together I swear that I will change. I'm begging you, please, help me to change, I understand if you don't want to get back together with me because, as I said, I'm a shit and I don't deserve you. You deserve to be happy because you are the most important thing in my life, and if you are happy, then so am I. If you don't want to answer me, then don't text back. I love you so much, you are my world. ♥. 22:41
Hey . . . man . . . Are you online and just not answering me? What a shitshow. 22:45
I try to do things right and even then I don't do it. Clearly, I'm an arsehole. 22:47
Message
This is harassment.
This is all manipulation and victimization, leaving the decision in your hands, so that you go back to him out of guilt.
This is not love, it is addiction, dependence, and obsession.
He thinks he is now aware of the problem, but he is not.
This is holding the other person responsible for the change.
This is a victim mentality.
This is lying.
This demonstrates that he is still controlling.
Victim mentality and manipulation, continuing the guilt trip.

So, swallowing your pride, you meet with your partner, intending to hear their apology. You're not thinking of getting back together. He doesn't deserve you.

When you meet, the conversation flows and you clearly state, point by point, all the things that the other person did wrong. You go on to self-criticize, and finally you make up.

When you get home, inexplicably, all that magical thinking we saw in the honeymoon phase reappears. "[. . .] you believe that this person is the love of your life. You feel that your bond is special, magical, and better than any other relationship you've ever had before [. . .]"

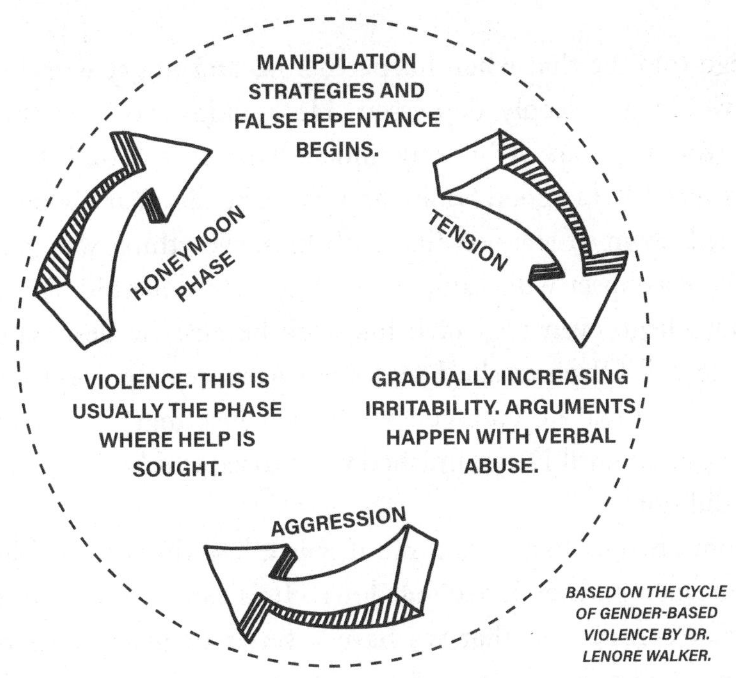

BASED ON THE CYCLE OF GENDER-BASED VIOLENCE BY DR. LENORE WALKER.

These phases are repeated time and time again. Over time, the tension phase shortens, the honeymoon phase almost disappears, and the aggression phase becomes permanent, culminating, if the bond is not broken beforehand, in physical aggression.

EMOTIONAL STABILITY DEPENDS ON THE PARTNER

Diego told me that when his partner became angry with him, he would get deeply depressed. He couldn't work or study. He would go out of his way and do whatever it took to get back into Olaya's good books, and when he did, that's when he calmed down. If she was fine with him, everything was good. If she was upset with him, everything went downhill. At one point, Diego even neglected his work because he desperately had to call Olaya as she'd said she was extremely upset with him. Olaya had no emergency. She was just angry. She could have waited until Diego finished work to express her anger, but she did not.

Some people have asked me if it is a bad thing to feel low when your partner is feeling down. It is not bad, it is quite normal considering that we have a series of neurons in the brain called *mirror neurons*, which allow us to feel empathy for others. But it's one thing for me to empathize with my partner or to be upset because we've just had an argument (it would be strange to be overjoyed after a situation like that), and quite another for my whole life to depend on how my partner feels. Diego's world stopped, as you have just seen, every time Olaya threw a tantrum. It was all but impossible for him to do anything else but attend to her. He couldn't concentrate or focus his attention on anything else.

CONSTANT NEED FOR AFFECTION, REASSURANCE, AND ATTENTION

In a healthy relationship, Olaya would not have told Diego that she was cross by text while he was at work, she would have waited until he got home and had the time to pay attention to her emotional needs. If Diego didn't answer because he was busy, and he let Olaya know this, this infuriated her further. Being with her forced him to keep an eye on his phone all the time and to be at her beck and call. She needed constant attention and didn't understand the boundaries that her partner was setting for her. None of Diego's attempts to show that, whatever happened, he would always be there, were enough for her. Sometimes, by way of protest, when he didn't meet her expectations, she would turn off her phone so that he would worry about her even more. This, for Diego, was a crushing form of punishment that truly made him believe he was letting her down, so he would then double down on giving her more attention, thus unintentionally reinforcing her behavior. This was Olaya's very passive-aggressive way of manipulating her boyfriend into always doing what she wanted.

We could say that Olaya's behavior was possibly driven by her idea of a relationship being based on some of those romantic love myths such as "love is when two become one" and "being in love means being together all the time and sharing everything."

However, let's concentrate for a moment on this protest behavior. I want to dive into detail on what it actually is.

Protest behavior is a cry for attention borne out of pain, arising out of the distress caused by separation from a loved one and the subsequent feelings of abandonment. Its existence can be explained in evolutionary terms, and can even be seen right from birth, as babies cry inconsolably upon being separated from their primary caregivers (father or mother), until contact is re-established with that parent. Indeed, it seems we continue resorting to this tool in adulthood.

It's understandable that during childhood we would engage in protest behaviors as we have not yet learned more effective communication strategies, however as adults we shouldn't resort to these tactics, we should rather know how to communicate our emotional needs in a more assertive manner. But, clearly, here we are faced with the problem of a lack of affective-sexual education. It is understandable not to be born with this knowledge, but it is admittedly also complicated to pick up on the fly.

I see protest behaviors in all types of relationships in my clinic, almost always maladaptively applied. They are essentially like taking an eye for an eye. They come from a place of hurt pride. "Oh, so you won't listen to me? Right, well, you'll see, I'll give you the cold shoulder and then you'll miss me. You'll soon come running back." This is what it boils down to, essentially. Thanks to their protest behavior, the person succeeds in receiving the attention they need, although in a very dysfunctional way (it could be described as a very subtle form of manipulation). This is what was happening between Diego and Olaya.

I can give you a couple more examples of protest behavior within this relationship. Let's see them in action in the following WhatsApp conversation.

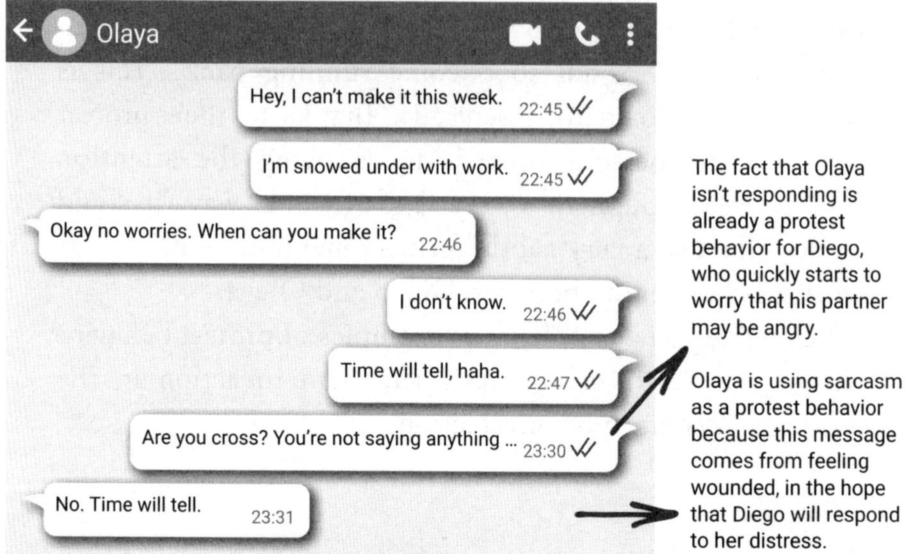

This is protest behavior because Olaya was not honest about how she felt about Diego's response, which, even if it was a joke, could have been a little clearer so as not to make her feel abandoned at that moment.

If either of these other two situations had occurred instead, perhaps there would have been no drama.

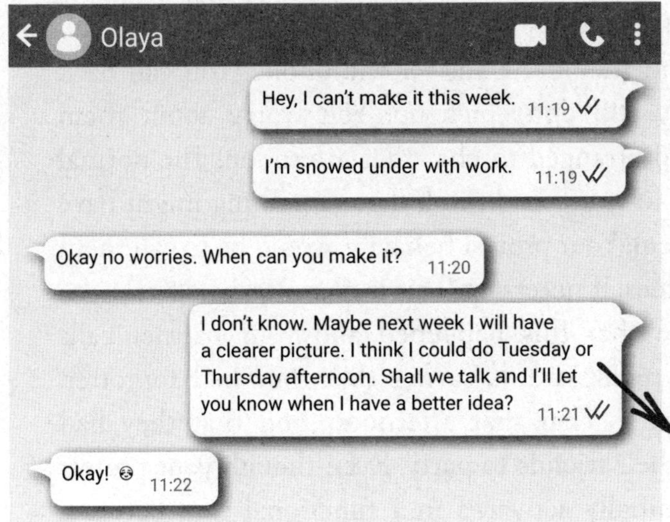

Diego knows Olaya and knows that uncertainty about the relationship and the future upsets her, so he tries to make the future as clear as possible whenever it is in his power to do so.

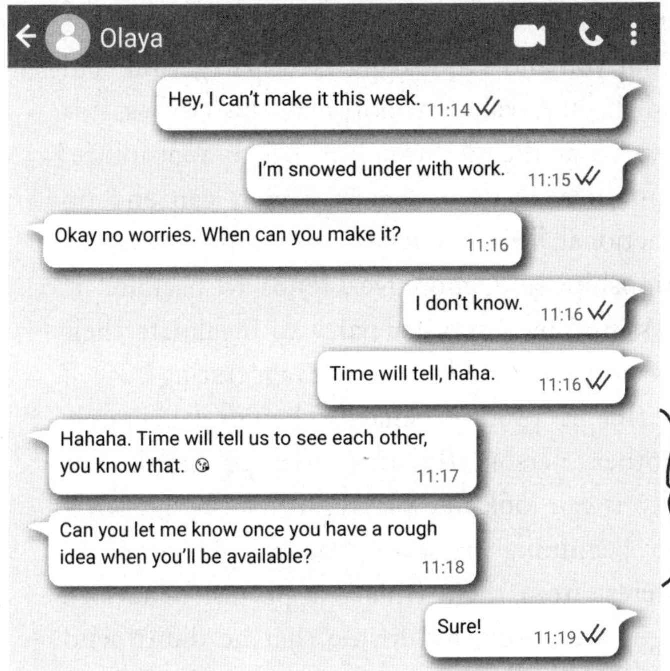

Olaya takes the comment lightheartedly and, instead of engaging in protest behavior caused by hurt pride, she confronts that pain by applying herself to proposing a solution.

Some protest behaviors are adaptive. Imagine that you call your partner and they don't answer the phone. You call back again, and they still don't pick up. You worry about them because you had arranged to chat that afternoon. The normal thing would be to worry and think that something might have happened to them. Your protest behavior would be to call them up to twenty times, if necessary. This is completely logical.

Now imagine that this happened and your partner calls you that same night, drunk, saying that they had forgotten you were meant to chat that afternoon, and that they had gone out with their friends to party. Even though your protest behavior was initially activated in a functional way, between the enormous dissonance of those contradictory messages from the partner ("I promise to call you because I love you, but then I forgot about you and I'm leaving for a party," and "I'm leaving you") and the ambivalent atmosphere this creates, it is likely to be activated at the slightest hint of "disappearance" of the partner on subsequent occasions, and it can end up becoming dysfunctional. This is a very common occurrence in dependent relationships and, moreover, tends to backfire. It is also sometimes used by the other party to invalidate their partner's feelings with phrases like "you're exaggerating".

A variant of this is protest behavior being deliberately induced in another person (lifelong manipulation). For example: typically, it can look like playing it cool by ignoring someone at the beginning of a relationship, in order to stir up more interest from them (this is a protest behavior). I once knew a guy who admitted to me that he didn't send me a message until three days after we first met because he thought it would make me keener to hear from him. *Logic not found*, but that's what he did. It did get under my skin because

I wondered why he hadn't messaged me, and I started to think that maybe he didn't even like me. It's unbelievable how abandoned I already felt, even though we hadn't even gone out together at that point. Needless to say, that relationship started out on completely the wrong footing, with me feeling beneath him, and with him feeling superior and controlling the situation, pulling the strings as if I were his puppet, even before we actually became a couple. We'll call this guy Matt. I'll tell you lots more about him later, and yes, you're going to freak out when you hear it, if you haven't already.

There was also a guy in my life who had the nerve to say that he wouldn't pay me any more attention (even though I had asked him directly to do so), because he thought it would make me too demanding. What a joke. Fortunately, this one came along when I was an adult, and I showed him the door right away.

Here are a few more examples of dysfunctional protest behavior:

Desperately trying to make contact:

Making intensive and inordinate attempts to establish contact by all means possible, for no apparent urgent reason. Calling, sending messages, attempting to get in touch via social media, either directly or indirectly, giving likes, leaving comments, or viewing content that they can see you have viewed, walking past their workplace, house, or an area where they might go to meet their friends, to see if you can "casually" bump into the other person. As you can see, there's a very fine line between dysfunctional protest behavior and harassment.

Keeping score:

That is, always waiting for the other person to make a move first, before matching it.

For example, analyzing how long your calls last or how long it takes them to reply to messages, so that you can "match their energy", or thinking: "If I go to the airport to pick you up today because you need it, I expect you to take me to work tomorrow, even if I don't need it, because otherwise the relationship will feel unbalanced."

Keeping score like this is about controlling the amount of give and take in the relationship down to the nth degree.

Deliberately stirring up jealousy:

Intentionally making the other person feel jealous so that they will care more about the relationship and pay you the attention you need.

1. Saying that an ex-partner has written to say that they are still in love with you.

Translation: "I'm so irresistible that my exes find me unforgettable. Look what I'm worth, you should value me more."

2. Asking your partner to join you for a few drinks with your ex.

Translation: "I'm saying this lightheartedly because, look, although I'm asking you to come, my intention is not really for you to come at all, because I know you won't want to; what I actually want is to show that you could lose me, to see if you'll wake up and smell the coffee."

This example reminds me of the film *The Break-Up* with Jennifer Aniston and Vince Vaughn. In this film the protagonists are a separated couple who are still living together in the same house. She parades her dates with other guys in front of her ex to make him feel jealous. Protest behavior disguised as romance to win back a partner by hurting them. How ironic. This could well be manipulation.

This leads us to another very common example in relationships that end:

3. Exaggeratedly showing off how well you're doing after the breakup, particularly on social media, with the aim of letting your ex-partner see how good things are for you without them (when in reality this is not true).

Translation: As in the previous example, this protest behavior is a way of saying "Hey, look how great I am doing without you. Can you see? I'm portraying myself in such a good light because I want you to see what you're missing, I want to hurt you, I want you to miss me, and I want us to get back in contact with each other."

Lying as a way to take revenge:

Vengeful lying, by saying things like you are busy and already have plans, so that when they ask you to meet up, you can't.

Translation: "See? Moving on from me has consequences."

Stonewalling:

Giving someone the silent treatment, the cold shoulder, and ignoring the other person. That is to say, engaging in behaviors which are typical of icing another person out. We will return to the topic of stonewalling later on.

Subtly threatening the other person by showing anger or the intention to leave to see if they will react and run after you:

For example, saying that you are not angry and hanging up the phone in the hope that your partner will call you back and say that they love you.

These behaviors are culturally reinforced by phrases like "if they wanted to, they would" which in themselves ring true, but which in the wrong context can give rise to dysfunctional behaviors and beliefs about love and relationships.

So, to summarize, protest behavior can be adaptive or maladaptive, depending on the circumstances, but in relationships featuring problematic dependence it almost always shows up as a maladaptive behavior.

Power struggles during conflict:

We have learned that arguing is about us being right and trying to prove someone else wrong, but it is not. That is not what arguing is about at all. An argument is a discussion, an opportunity to voice a problem, express emotions, empathize, ask for forgiveness, and if necessary, find solutions, negotiate and solve the problem, leaving entirely to one side whichever one of you is right or wrong, because that only creates distance between people. Clashing like this is a great opportunity to get to know your partner and for your partner to get to know you. It's a chance for the couple to actually build closer emotional bonds. Conflicts aren't about apportioning blame; they're about finding solutions and learning.

And if you don't think so, you haven't learned how to argue properly.

When a problem crops up in the relationship, there are two possible ways to handle it. One is to consider the other person a part of the problem, and the other is to face the problem headlong together, as a team. The first option leads us to view our partner as the enemy, thus creating a power struggle along the lines of "who can do more" or "who is more right", in which both empathy and self-awareness may have flown out of the window.

Olaya, instead of finding peaceful refuge in Diego as someone to confide in, paid the cost of her emotional damage with the one person she considered to be the source of her discontent.

Diego once got angry with her for arriving late to an appointment and Olaya turned indignant. She perceived the criticism as a personal attack and, offended, she insinuated to Diego that if he didn't want to be with her, then he should just say so.

> "Oh, man, I'm so sorry," she said. "There was traffic ... as if you have never been late before. Come on, if you are so angry . . . I'll leave if that's what you want."
>
> "No, no, it's not that," answered Diego. "I just think you could have told me, that's all."
>
> "I couldn't because I was driving."
>
> "Yeah, but ... Whatever."

At this point it would have been great if Olaya had said "Okay, I know, you're right. Please forgive me. I couldn't warn you because I was driving, but I apologize because it's true that you must've been waiting here for a while on your own. That wasn't my intention. Can I buy you a drink to make up for it?" She could have handled it like a queen, rising above the problem, and aligned with Diego. But no, that's not what happened.

"No, so now it's my fault that you've been stuck here waiting," she spat.

"I didn't say that."

"No, but you implied it. Like so many other times. You always do this. At the end of the day, I'm always the bad guy. Well, you know what? If you don't like it, you can go out with someone else."

And so, once again, Diego and Olaya were in the midst of more "drama".

After the relationship's slide downhill, Olaya and Diego, as you already know, started talking again and managed to reconcile. The never-ending story.

IDEALIZING THE PARTNER

"I will never find anyone like him", "She is perfect. She's the whole package", "If I leave him, I will never be happy", and so on. These are just a few of the phrases which reflect how some people idealize their partners.

The cons of idealizing someone are:

- It is easier for your thoughts, your emotions, your behavior, and your life to revolve around that person.
- You find it very difficult to set boundaries.
- When things start to go wrong, you are more reluctant to distance yourself from that person.
- You have a much harder time getting over a breakup.
- When you realize that things are not going how you thought they were, it comes as a big shock.

My gosh, I idealized my partner so much that even after the breakup, I needed to find similarities with my ex in all the rest of the men I was meeting.

CONSTANTLY NEEDING TO KNOW WHAT THE PARTNER IS DOING

A few years ago, I heard the story of Julia, a 29-year-old woman who was in a relationship with Nate, 31. I never met him, but Julia told me that, after he was unfaithful to her, they both got used to sharing their locations every time they left the house. It's interesting that during this session Julia defended the idea that this gesture implied transparency on Nate's behalf, and that this increased her confidence in him.

"Julia, trust between a couple isn't built that way," I said to her in the first session. "Trust in a partner is, practically speaking, a leap of faith. You trust that the other person loves you and will be there for you. To have faith means there is no need for demonstrations like this. That's why it is so hard to regain trust after infidelity. If the process were as easy as the other person simply being transparent, there would be no need for therapy at all, don't you think?"

"Well, yes, but then how can I trust Nate again after what he did to me?"

"First, you have to get over what happened, and for that you need to process and grieve. Then you need to, with your partner, try to go back and recreate that same environment of emotional stability that you two had before, at the same time, we'll work together on tackling those recurrent thoughts spinning around in your head and driving you crazy. Anything less than this will just lead you to feel suspicious, and believe me, that, in the long run, can turn your bond into something toxic. To do this, as a couple, we'll get you working on your communication style, how you show affection, and on spending time together, among other things."

"That doesn't sound easy."

"It's not. I'm not going to lie to you."

After that conversation, many more things spilled out. Julia not only used his location to build "trust", but from time to time she also checked Nate's phone and stalked his social media to feel that she had some level of control over the relationship. Julia managed her emotions by controlling her environment, but that was not a good solution.

EMOTIONAL EXHAUSTION AND FEELING LIKE YOU ARE SUFFERING

When you're in the middle of a dependent relationship, it can feel as if you are pulling against the tide. There is so much anxiety, uncertainty, and suffering, all the time. You may feel absolutely spent, like you can't keep going, but you still keep picking yourself up and trying to pull in the right direction, as Clara put it.

Toxic relationships keep you constantly on your toes, on high alert, for whatever might happen, which equates to a chronic activation of the sympathetic nervous system (this is the part of the nervous system which activates when the brain senses danger and anticipates that you will have to defend yourself).

To make matters worse, the couple's close family and friends may be able to intuit that all is not rosy in the relationship, which may be perceived and interpreted by the couple as "everyone is against our love", that "they are all just jealous of what we have", or that "we have to keep fighting because we love each other, and nothing can come between us", thus reinforcing certain magical beliefs in order to stay in their little *Twilight* or *Fifty Shades of Grey* bubble.

SEX AS A "MUST" FOR INTIMACY

This is something that absolutely frustrates me. To be clear, I'm not talking about rape, but rather the problematic view of sex as an obligation and a mere transaction. This mindset is unacceptable and needs to be challenged.

There are some people, mostly women, who feel that they "have to do it". They believe that if their partner is not satisfied, they will go elsewhere to satisfy their sexual needs with someone else (as if sex were a physiological need like eating or sleeping). In some way, they feel forced to submit, perhaps not directly by their partner, but by our culture's ingrained belief in the importance of male sexual satisfaction, in order for the marriage to last. Married or not, even in the 21st century, many women (and some men) still feel this pressure.

Then there is another narrative that I also love (note the sarcasm). It's the thought of "owing" someone sex. Yes, you read that right. Have you ever gone out for dinner and drinks with someone and ended up feeling like you owed them something? Especially if that person has invited you to dinner or drinks (or both).

I've occasionally heard phrases like "Are you really going to leave me like this?"

Someone whom I once mentioned this feeling to said, "Do it if you want to, and if you don't want to, then just don't." Of course, yes, but that's not what I'm getting at. I'm referring to a particular behavior that is somehow implicit in dating someone you like (yet another kind of unwritten rule).

I've written on this subject in my book *Ama tu sexo [Love Your Sex]*, showing examples of phrases which might be used to blackmail and manipulate someone into having sex. But I'll also leave these little gems here, to give you more of an idea what I'm talking about:

"If we do it, our relationship will be stronger."

Reality check: Having sex does not make a relationship stronger, just as not having sex doesn't weaken it. Sex is just one way of expressing affection, amongst many, it certainly isn't the only one.

"When we haven't had sex in a long time, I feel you don't love me that much."

Reality check: The frequency of sexual intercourse also has no correlation with love.

And that's when manipulation isn't associated with pressure not to use condoms, with threats to call the relationship off if not, which can look like this:

"If you really loved me, we'd do it without a condom."

Reality check: To say this is like comparing apples to oranges.

"If you trusted me, you'd believe I was clean, and we could do it without a condom."

Reality check: No matter how much you trust a person, trust is not an STI test or a barrier method.

To go without a condom, you must consider something else besides unwanted pregnancy: sexually transmitted infections. To have sex without a condom with someone, it must be an exclusive (closed) relationship, and you should have been with that person for at least a year (due to the length of the incubation period for some infections, such as HIV). After this year, it is advisable for both of you to have blood tests to check for sexually transmitted infections. If all is well, then you can have sex without a condom.

I would also like to take this opportunity to talk about stealthing, which refers to taking off the condom in the middle of a sexual encounter. This practice is a sexual assault if the encounter was consented to on the basis that a condom would be used.

So, remember: sex requires consent, consensus, and the freedom to choose whether to do it or not. Under coercion, blackmail, or manipulation, it is sexual abuse.

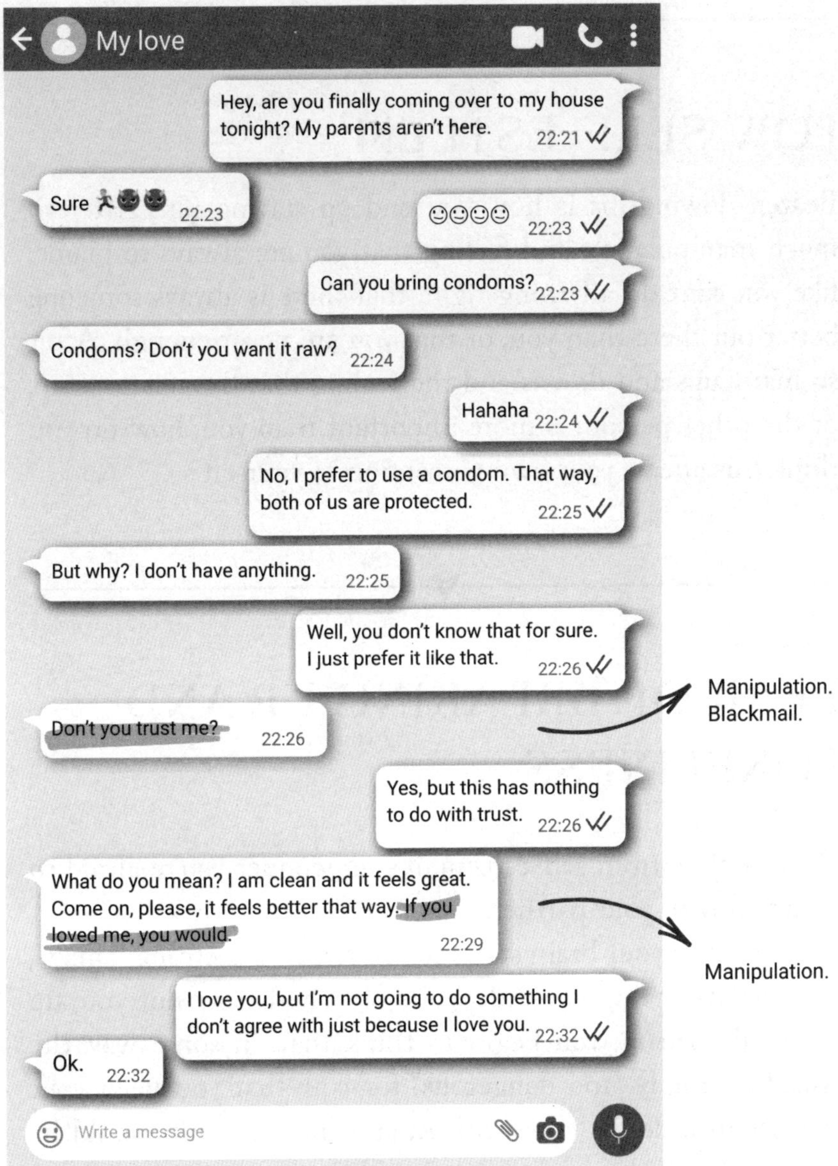
My love
Hey, are you finally coming over to my house tonight? My parents aren't here. 22:21
Sure 22:23
22:23
Can you bring condoms? 22:23
Condoms? Don't you want it raw? 22:24
Hahaha 22:24
No, I prefer to use a condom. That way, both of us are protected. 22:25
But why? I don't have anything. 22:25
Well, you don't know that for sure. I just prefer it like that. 22:26
Don't you trust me? 22:26
Yes, but this has nothing to do with trust. 22:26
What do you mean? I am clean and it feels great. Come on, please, it feels better that way. If you loved me, you would. 22:29
I love you, but I'm not going to do something I don't agree with just because I love you. 22:32
Ok. 22:32
Write a message
Manipulation. Blackmail.
Manipulation.

LOW SELF-ESTEEM

Beaten down. This is how you end up staying put. After so much manipulation and feeling that you are always to blame, like you can't do anything right, that there is always someone better out there than you, or that you are never enough. After so many ups and downs and the feeling that the relationship, or the other person, is more important than you, how do you think this affects your own perception of yourself?

FEAR OF BREAKING UP AND LONELINESS

With rock bottom self-esteem, it's no wonder you're afraid to break up with your partner.

As soon as your brain starts to see you as something "small", and that your happiness depends on whether or not you are with this person, you begin to think that, in some way, the world is simply "too dangerous" for you, that you need your partner in order to cope with it, and that your life would be meaningless if they are not by your side.

But if your happiness depends on that person, then it's not your happiness.

♥ 5 ♥

AFFECTIVE RESPONSIBILITY

Before we delve a little deeper into dependent relationships, I want to discuss a concept that is just as important, but little understood: affective responsibility.

When we talk about affective responsibility, we are talking about being aware that what we say and do (or what we don't say and do) has an impact on others. In a relationship, taking affective responsibility is all about respecting both your own and your partner's needs and emotions, being aware of them right from the start, when the bond is first formed. This means that the concept must be practiced in a couple relationship (or even within a friendship or family relationship) right from the very beginning, because, although you may not officially be dating at that stage, even early on you are not "nothing" either. If there is a baseline intention to create intimacy at any level, then the duty to demonstrate affective responsibility therefore exists.

AFFECTIVE RESPONSIBILITY LOOKS LIKE THIS:

- Talking about one's own feelings and respecting those of the other person.
- Practicing assertiveness and empathy.
- Making relationship intentions and expectations abundantly clear.
- Working on good communication skills.
- Talking about what bothers you.
- Negotiating and respecting the boundaries being set in the relationship.
- Reaching agreements and being able to modify them as the relationship progresses.
- Taking care of each other.

- Understanding that our actions have consequences on the other person.
- Validating the other person's emotions.
- Ensuring consent and consensus for sexual activities.

WHAT AFFECTIVE RESPONSIBILITY IS NOT:

- Taking responsibility for the other person's emotions.

The principle of fairness: It is okay if we sometimes worry slightly more about our partner because, for example, they may be having emotional problems or they're not in good spirits at certain times in their life. However, it's not healthy to tip the balance over to one side like this on a regular basis because this means we're living "for" the other person.

- Withholding important information about our feelings from the other person.
- Invalidating the partner's emotions. (We'll go into this in more depth later.)
- Failing to respect negotiated boundaries or not understanding that people may change their minds over time, as the relationship develops.
- Engaging in behaviors which may lead the other person on while having no real intention to get more involved in a relationship.
- Blaming your partner for your own feelings.
- Presuming that, without communication, emotions, feelings, or thoughts can be guessed.

- Ghosting someone, e.g.: "We were going to have a date this weekend, but, since we're not together, I think I'll pass. I won't tell him though."

SINCERITY AND BRUTAL HONESTY

I mentioned earlier that affective responsibility includes being honest with your partner about your feelings. I'd like to take a brief detour on this subject because, even though I believe honesty is important in a relationship, not everything goes. I think we can distinguish between two distinct concepts: sincerity and brutal honesty.

A SINCERE PERSON ...

- Filters what they say.
- Knows that it's not always necessary to say exactly what they're thinking.
- Communicates assertively.
- Acts ethically.
- Reflects on their behavior.
- Understands that other people may have different points of view from their own.
- Picks an appropriate time to express their opinions.
- Acts thoughtfully.
- Uses non-hurtful words.

A BRUTALLY HONEST PERSON ...

- Behaves impulsively.
- Communicates aggressively.
- Confuses opinion with truth.
- Believes that their own opinion is the absolute truth.
- Is capable of being hurtful to others.
- Considers themselves honest because they say things to a person's face.
- Has no filter when they speak.
- Does not measure the impact of their own words.
- Always speaks their mind.

Clearly, being sincere is consistent with taking affective responsibility, however being brutally honest is not.

To demonstrate this a bit more clearly, I'll give you an example of what it looks like to be sincere, on the one hand, and brutally honest on the other, within a relationship.

YOU ARE BEING SINCERE WHEN:

- You are in a relationship, but you have developed feelings for someone else, and you tell your partner.
- You want to end the relationship and you sit down to talk to your partner about it.
- You are cross with your partner, and you tell them in a calm and respectful manner.
- An ex-partner, who you once loved, reaches out to you on social media, after a long time. You would quite like to meet up with this person, and, although you no longer have feelings for them, you tell your partner anyway in case it would bother them.

YOU ARE BEING BRUTALLY HONEST WHEN:

- When talking about your past to your partner, you regale them with all the intimate sexual details of the things you did with other people, under the pretext of letting them get to know you better, sexually speaking.
- **Why is this considered brutally honest?** Because there is no need to do this. Talking about the sexual details of your past is unnecessary for your partner to get to know you. You can talk about your sexual tastes without having to say with whom you did what, and when, or why.
- You want to end the relationship, so you send a WhatsApp message to your partner to tell them clearly, so that the weight of this decision is off your shoulders.
- **Why is this considered brutally honest?** Because issues this important, which affect other people, shouldn't take place via a WhatsApp conversation. This comes across as very impersonal and communicates a certain disregard for both the subject and the person you're speaking to. Also, it can lead to misunderstandings. Leaving a relationship, although there is a cost, can't be treated the same way as letting someone know you're nipping to the shop. It is not just a daily chore to be ticked off the to-do list. We must set aside the proper time and space to be fair to ourselves and to the other person.
- You're cross with your partner and you tell them so, without any kind of filter, bluntly speaking your truth because you are honest, and if they don't like it, tough. It is what it is.
- **Why is this considered brutally honest?** Because it's not all about speaking your mind and getting everyone to agree with you. Your "truth" is not absolute.
- A past love reaches out to you through social media after a long period of time and, although you feel nothing for this person anymore, you tell your partner.

- **Why is this considered brutally honest?** Because if this is inconsequential to the relationship and to you, then in the context of your own relationship it is unnecessary information. Telling your partner may be more costly than beneficial (for example, you might cause your partner to freak out for no reason).
- You have sexual fantasies about other people you know, and you tell them to your partner.
- **Why is this considered brutally honest?** Because your partner doesn't need to know all your sexual fantasies, especially if they involve people you know. This could lead your partner to develop insecurities if they don't understand the concept. Indeed, some couples do share their sexual fantasies, but it's unnecessary to have an outburst of sincerity (or rather, brutal honesty) to do so.

♥ 6 ♥

HOW TO IDENTIFY EMOTIONAL ABUSE

Emotional abuse is psychological mistreatment and can begin in the most subtle of ways. We have also normalized it so much that, most of the time, not only do we fail to realize when it's happening, but if we do realize what's going on and point it out, we receive a counter-explanation from family or friends as to why what we're pointing out is, in fact, an expression of love.

This romanticization of emotional abuse paves the way for easy escalation into physical abuse. Even without necessarily reaching this fateful point, it is well known that the consequences of emotional abuse can be terrible due to the psychological wounds inflicted on the person on the receiving end.

In a moment, I will go through the behaviors which can be considered emotional abuse within relationships one by one. What I'm hoping to do with this is help you to identify these behaviors in your day-to-day life. This knowledge can give you the power to understand what is happening, so that, consequently, you can react and take whatever action you deem necessary.

STONEWALLING

"Stonewalling" is the word we use to describe a range of behaviors aimed at ignoring a partner.

It is the most passive-aggressive form of emotional abuse in existence.

It happens when one person in the relationship thinks that the other has done something "wrong". They become angry about it, and, instead of talking it out, they ignore their partner, acting coldly towards them, being emotionally distant, and generally displaying a lack of empathy. Effectively, the partner is being "punished" with the silent treatment.

EXAMPLES OF STONEWALLING:

- No longer replying to messages.
- Disregarding what their partner says.
- Overlooking expressed requests or needs.
- Pretending they can't hear.
- Not answering questions or giving monosyllabic answers.
- Acting as if the other person is invisible.
- Avoiding physical touch and eye contact.
- Showing disinterest in what the other person says or does.
- Not coming to social events or canceling plans.
- Not showing affection and consciously ignoring the other person's expressed emotional distress or suffering.

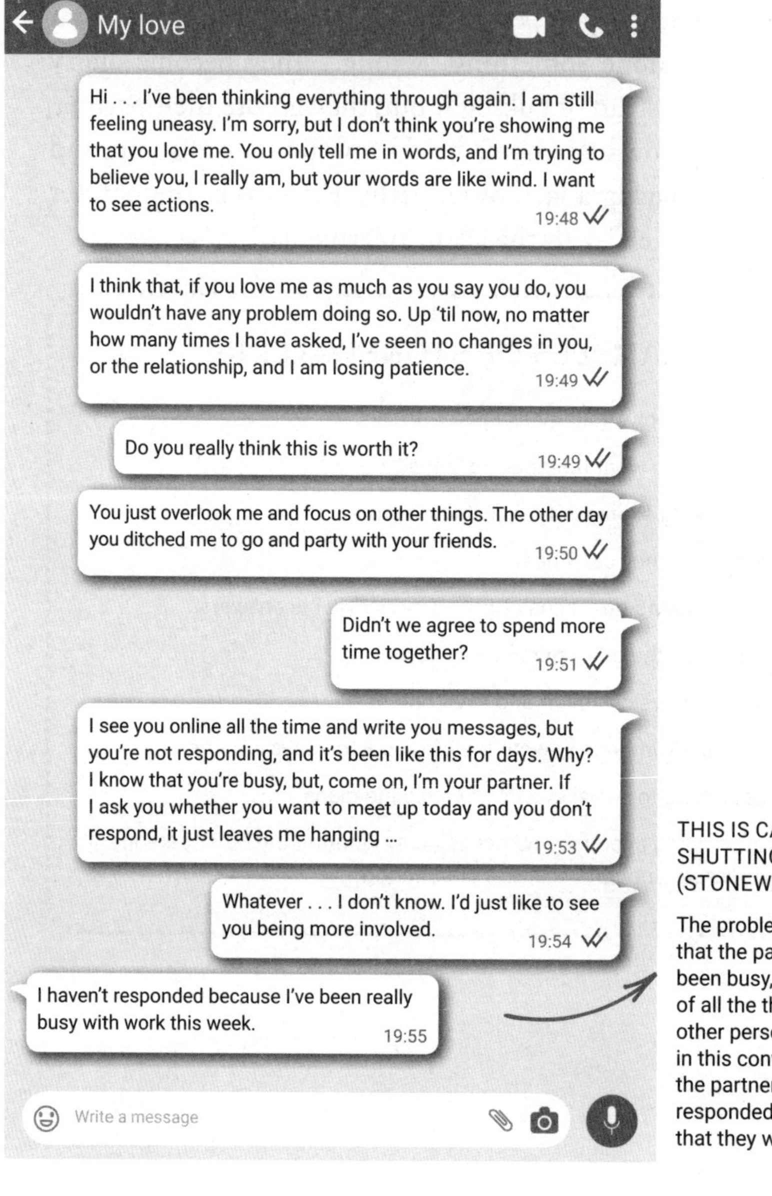

THIS IS CALLED SHUTTING DOWN (STONEWALLING).

The problem isn't that the partner has been busy, it's that, of all the things the other person has said in this conversation, the partner has only responded to the bit that they want to.

This behavior, typical of stonewalling, is called shutting down. It is when a person ignores messages or behaviors that don't interest them.

In the previous example, we see how the person completely ignores the entirety of the message and only responds to the complaint about not having replied to the WhatsApp messages. This can drive the other person to completely lose their cool, feeling misunderstood and/or frustrated. A person responding like this, by ignoring everything else, is attempting to justify their disappearance with an argument which is difficult for the other person to disprove and easy for the sender to defend. "What do you mean you don't understand that I've been busy? I have a right to a life. Don't keep on at me." But, that, as you may have seen, is clearly not the focus of the actual problem at hand. However, the message recipient might well think something like "Okay, it's true, he has a right to have a life. Maybe I'm being a pain. Although I still feel bad about all the rest." And, boom, the manipulation is done ("the fuss", as one of my patients calls it). This story could go on, with the message sender feeling angry and misunderstood, aggressively repeating all the things that haven't been answered, and the message recipient invalidating that anger with phrases such as "It's not that big a deal", or dismissing it as exaggerated or crazy because of the way the sender is communicating. Later on, we will name and discuss this form of manipulation in detail.

The person who is shutting down might do so because the message they're ignoring seems unimportant to them, or perhaps because they do not personally have the skills or arguments to adequately respond. They may simply prefer to avoid any feelings of discomfort by not providing the expected response. Their main objective is simply to make the other person's behavior, which is bothering them, disappear.

The consequences can be terrible:

FOR THE RELATIONSHIP:

- This cultivates a poor capacity to resolve conflict.
- Uncommunicated problems then become entrenched.
- The quality of any communication which does take place is very poor.
- This situation can encourage the development of a level of emotional dependence, given that stonewalling may be considered a form of punishment (also, giving mixed signals and intermittent reinforcement).

FOR THE VICTIM:

- Uncertainty, stress, anxiety, and sadness.
- Low self-esteem and insecurity. They may ask themselves what happened, or what they may have done wrong this time.
- Having the feeling that something isn't right. As the other person isn't talking or saying anything, there is no way to address the situation or obtain clarity on what's actually going on.
- Constant worry (which, as you know, increases the probability of developing codependence).
- Neglecting to live their own life or avoiding old behaviors, for fear of making the other person angry.

I have lots to say about this from my own personal experience.

The relationship in which I was most affected by stonewalling was the one I had with Aaron. I learned what to say and what not to say purely on the basis of what might upset him. Neither being assertive nor unassertive. There were simply things that I couldn't say, comment on, or bring up. I learned it all through trial and error. Every time I confronted him about something he did that bothered me, he would disappear off the face of the earth. He would ignore my comment and just start talking about other things, or he would completely ghost me, disappearing for days.

Ghosting is the practice of cutting communication or contact with a partner, friend, or any other person to whom you have an affective responsibility, without prior warning. It is also known as "leaving someone on 'read'" or simply ignoring the other person. Aaron ignored me. I told you it would happen. One time, this went on for a whole three weeks. It was his way of punishing me for having brought up a subject which was uncomfortable for him, or for having done something which, according to him, was wrong.

Do you remember what I said about affective responsibility and not shouldering the responsibility for other people's emotions? Well, that was exactly what I did. I didn't abide by the principle of fairness when it comes to affective responsibility. I lived directly for him. If something made him feel bad, to avoid the punishment of not having him, I would stop doing it. When I saw that he, on the contrary, praised me or praised someone else for doing or saying something specific, I would repeat it to gain his approval. I was modifying all my own behavior.

The practice of ghosting is a passive-aggressive behavior which demonstrates a failure to comply with the expectations around affective responsibility in the relationship, regardless of the relationship's status. It shows a complete lack of respect, but specifically, a lack of respect regarding a person's affective responsibility towards the other.

How can someone simply choose to disappear, without explanation? We could hypothesize on the various possible causes, such as:

- Perhaps they have a fear of commitment (they may potentially see commitment or the relationship in a very dysfunctional light, as if it were a trap or an environment where they will be forced to give up their independence and constantly have to explain themselves). Or they may fear being emotionally hurt if they establish emotional intimacy or close ties, (remember, this is a fear that you WILL NOT be able to save them, neither with your affection, nor with the power of your love).
- Because they don't understand the concept of affective responsibility or don't know how to put it into action.
- Because they avoid facing up to situations which make them feel uncomfortable.
- And my favorite, because they have absolutely no interest in the relationship. We can only guess ...

It is much better to say something that makes it clear to the other person that you are not interested in the relationship, or that you are not willing to face up to something, rather than disappear as if you've fallen off the face of the earth.

HERE ARE SOME EXAMPLES OF THINGS YOU CAN SAY INSTEAD OF GHOSTING:

- I really enjoyed meeting you, but after our date I've been thinking it over, and I think we are looking for different things. I'd like to focus on looking for someone with whom I truly believe I can have a deeper connection.
- Unfortunately, I don't really have those feelings for you, and I would like to invest my time in finding someone who I do feel that way about.
- I don't think that we could be a couple in the future, but I do think you're really great and, if you're open to it, we could be friends and still go out for a drink together now and then, if we both feel comfortable with that. What do you think?
- I think you're an incredible person, but I think we see the world very differently. I would prefer us to stop being in contact. I wish all the best for you.
- I think I'm looking for something less serious, so I've been thinking that it would be best if we stop seeing each other. Otherwise, we could end up unintentionally hurting each other.
- I've been thinking long and hard about us, and I think it would be best if we part ways and follow our separate paths.
- I think I am looking for something more serious, so I've been thinking that it would be best if we stop seeing each other. Otherwise, we could end up unintentionally hurting each other.
- I need to talk to you about something important. I've really enjoyed our time together these last few days, but I have met someone else, and I would like to focus on that relationship.

With this, we can save the other person from suffering the typical effects of ghosting:

- Constantly checking to see if the other person has replied.
- Going round in circles thinking "What did I do wrong, for the other person to have just disappeared?"

- Decreased confidence in themselves.
- Low self-esteem.
- Emotional dependence.
- Anxiety.
- Doubting oneself and comparing oneself to others.

What happens if the person we say the above phrases to does not respect the boundary we are setting?

If you decide to break up with your partner, your friend with benefits, or the person with whom you were beginning to develop a certain degree of intimacy, and they do not respect that boundary, as ironic as it may sound, your only option at that point is to disappear. Blocking or no longer maintaining contact in this situation is not considered ghosting. Romantic relationships are not maintained through coercion or manipulation; they must be entered into freely. So, by their very nature, two people cannot stay together if one does not want to, which means that if there is no relationship, there is no affective responsibility.

We can only talk about ghosting when there is some level of intimate bond between two people and one of them disappears without explanation.

Following a breakup, there is no bond. Without a bond, there is no affective responsibility towards the other person, therefore, there is no disappearance, only a breakup.

WHAT CAN YOU DO IF SOMEONE GHOSTS YOU?

- If it has only happened once, I would recommend approaching the discussion calmly and with a sense of curiosity. Nobody is born knowing these things, and we all make mistakes. Hopefully, it would not then happen again.
- If it does happen again, I think at that point it's worth considering whether you are getting what you need out of the relationship. By that I don't mean simply considering whether the "good times" are worth it; there are good times in every relationship. I'm talking about doing a cost-benefit analysis to see whether, on balance, the relationship is coming down more heavily on one side or the other.

The 24-hour rule:

Some people do need time to process an argument by "disappearing". This isn't really a problem, as long as certain conditions are being met.

If you're one of those people who shuts down when faced with conflict in a relationship, or who finds it very hard to control your impulses, this rule is for you. If, when faced with a complex situation, you can feel yourself becoming overwhelmed, or you think you might lose your temper in the moment, try to wait a reasonable amount of time before responding. The only stipulation is that this length of time should be no longer than 24 hours. In the moment, try to relax.

If the conflict is with someone close to you, let them know that you will need a certain amount of time before you will be able to respond calmly, so that the other person is not left hanging, waiting and feeling uncertain, nor feeling "unacknowledged" by you. This latter point is really important so that the other person avoids suffering the consequences of stonewalling, and so that they don't end up thinking that you are ghosting them.

MANIPULATION

Manipulation is a form of control and emotional blackmail which aims to make the victim think, feel, or act, without realizing it, exactly as the manipulator wants.

The manipulator seeks, mainly, to neutralize any capacity for criticism, even self-criticism, by using strategies based on persuasion and suggestion. They may or may not be aware of what they're doing. I like to point this out because there are some people who engage in manipulation tactics without realizing that they are being manipulative, while there are others who manipulate with full knowledge and awareness of what they are doing. Unfortunately, the victim is never aware of it at first (unless they can recognize patterns of manipulation).

Manipulation is therefore very difficult to pinpoint, especially because manipulators do it so intelligently and very very subtly, mainly by alluding to their victim's weaknesses.

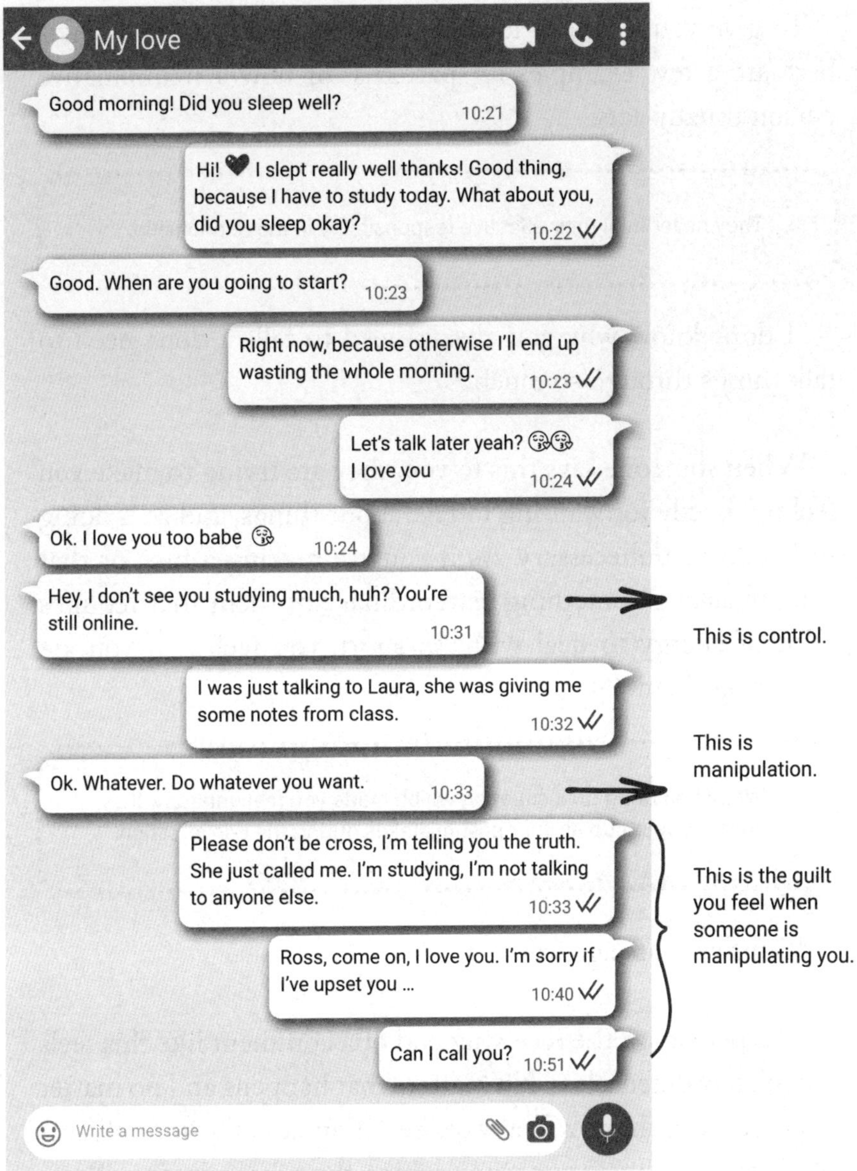

This is control.

This is manipulation.

This is the guilt you feel when someone is manipulating you.

To give you a clearer idea of what manipulation looks like, here are a few examples or "patterns" of how a manipulative person usually acts:

- They never fulfil their affective responsibility in the relationship.

"I don't know why you always need to talk. I don't need to talk things through so much."

When someone says this to you, they are trying to make you feel too needy for wanting to talk about things, and as if doing so is odd or unnecessary. As if you are making a fuss, or that you are asking something extraordinary of them that requires a lot of energy to deal with. In short, you feel as if you are bothering them.

- When you bring up a situation which made you feel unhappy, they start dredging up all your past mistakes during the conversation.

"But five years ago, you . . ."

The person on the receiving end of a comment like this feels completely defenseless. No matter what happens and no matter what you do, there will always be an apparently unforgivable black mark against your name, which the other person will use against you, like a weapon, any time you try to criticize their behavior. It's as if the person saying this to you is really saying "Your criticism is unwarranted, look, you've done worse in the past. Actually, I'm the victim here."

- When you don't do what they want, they give you the cold shoulder (stonewalling).
- They guilt-trip you in every argument or discussion ... They twist everything, turning the tables on you.

"I didn't like it when you did or said *X*."

"Do you think it's okay for you to say that to me while we're in the car?"

This is manipulation, because the important thing is not the fact that they are in the car. The manipulator is twisting things so that the most important part of the conversation becomes "the error" that the victim is committing by bringing this up in the car and trying to make them feel guilty for doing so. What the manipulator is trying to do here is to switch the focus of attention away from something important, for which they are likely somewhat responsible, and onto something unimportant, like the fact that they're trying to have this conversation in the car.

- They belittle you, or try to humiliate you, and then say they were "only joking".

"Hahaha, you look like a mole in those glasses." My first boyfriend said this to me. I've always had bad eyesight (inherited from my dad), and unfortunately, when I couldn't wear my contact lenses or while I was at home, I had to wear those infamous "bottle-bottom glasses". Bottle-bottom glasses, for those who don't know, have those thick lenses which make your eyes look like a pair of ping-pong balls.

I had already suffered enough, wearing those horrible glasses, without the person I loved throwing that insult at me "as a joke". Even though I told him that his supposed joke wasn't funny at all, and that it upset me, he clearly enjoyed humiliating me because he said it every time I put them on. As a result, I stopped wearing glasses in front of him as much as possible, even if that meant hardly being able to see, or not letting my eyes rest from the contact lenses.

You can't imagine how much it pains me to dig up all these old memories and lay them out for you here, in context, having now analyzed them properly.

- They tend to justify their behavior or opinions by referring to the opinions of third parties.

"I'm not the only one who thinks so."

As if other people's opinions were the gospel truth. The only thing this person is trying to do here is create pressure. What's more, when they say "I'm not the only one who thinks so", they almost always mean their friends, who, obviously, will only have heard their version of events and will probably take their side, because that's what friends are for.

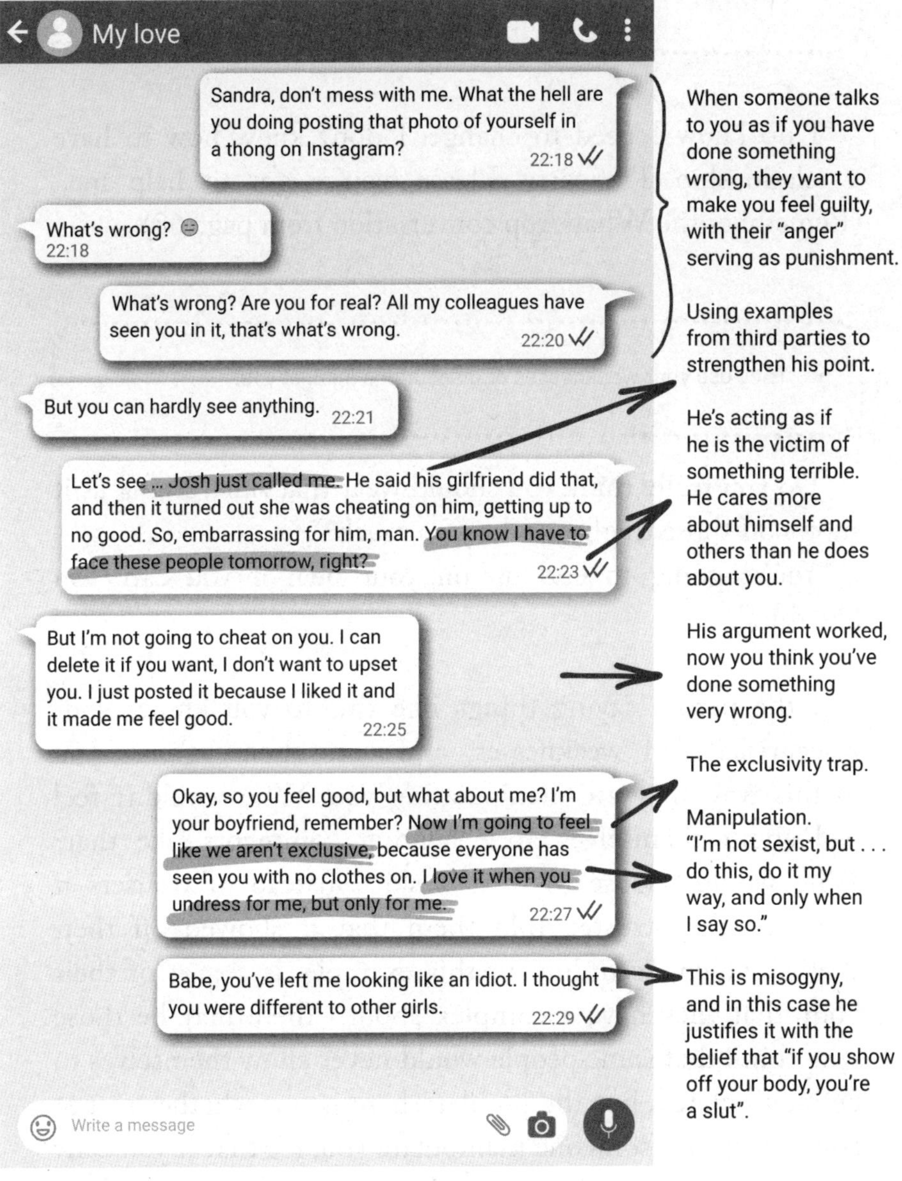
My love
Sandra, don't mess with me. What the hell are you doing posting that photo of yourself in a thong on Instagram? 22:18
What's wrong? 22:18
What's wrong? Are you for real? All my colleagues have seen you in it, that's what's wrong. 22:20
But you can hardly see anything. 22:21
Let's see ... Josh just called me. He said his girlfriend did that, and then it turned out she was cheating on him, getting up to no good. So, embarrassing for him, man. You know I have to face these people tomorrow, right? 22:23
But I'm not going to cheat on you. I can delete it if you want, I don't want to upset you. I just posted it because I liked it and it made me feel good. 22:25
Okay, so you feel good, but what about me? I'm your boyfriend, remember? Now I'm going to feel like we aren't exclusive, because everyone has seen you with no clothes on. I love it when you undress for me, but only for me. 22:27
Babe, you've left me looking like an idiot. I thought you were different to other girls. 22:29
Write a message
When someone talks to you as if you have done something wrong, they want to make you feel guilty, with their "anger" serving as punishment.
Using examples from third parties to strengthen his point.
He's acting as if he is the victim of something terrible. He cares more about himself and others than he does about you.
His argument worked, now you think you've done something very wrong.
The exclusivity trap.
Manipulation. "I'm not sexist, but . . . do this, do it my way, and only when I say so."
This is misogyny, and in this case he justifies it with the belief that "if you show off your body, you're a slut".

- They play the victim to make you feel sorry for them.

"I do know I need to change. I don't know how to have a relationship. I'm sorry. Please, you've got to help me." (Remember the WhatsApp conversation from page 68).

- They use your weaknesses or insecurities against you.

"Do you really think you should wear that skirt, seeing as it shows off those thighs you hate so much?"

"You're going to end up on your own if you carry on like this."

If the person saying things like this to you knows your insecurities and weaknesses, and uses them against you in this way, they are manipulating you. Who wouldn't feel bad about themselves after hearing comments like that? Who would choose to wear a skirt instead of trousers if someone they trusted told them that it showed off their thighs, which, according to this example, is a part of their body that they have a complex about? There may be those who think that some people would never allow themselves to be manipulated, but the problem here is not whether or not you would "let" someone manipulate you, it's that if you can't recognize manipulative tactics in the first place, then from the very first moment you will unwittingly become a victim, having never even had the opportunity to decide whether or not you would ever "allow yourself" to be manipulated. And therein lies the problem.

- They subtly threaten you.

"Are you really going to go out dressed like that? You'll make a fool of yourself."

When someone says something like this to you, envisaging a worst-case scenario about something you're doing, what they're really saying is that they want to do something else. Of course, common sense always applies.

- They hide hurtful remarks behind phrases like "I just worry about you".

"Do you really think that the best way to tackle this problem is *X*? I think you need to grow up a bit and stop thinking that life is all about posting your pics on social media. I'm only saying this because I'm worried about you, and I want to see you do well."

"I'm only so hard on you because I worry about you and I don't want to see you struggle."

- They use sarcasm to diminish what you do.

"You're going to study science? Whoever would have thought?"

Translation: "You? A stupid idiot like you, you think you can study science? That's only for smart people. I think you should do something else that doesn't involve the possibility of doing better professionally in life than me."

- Controlling what you wear and disguising it as "love".

"Have you noticed that people stare at your cleavage a lot? I don't have a problem with you wearing low-cut tops. I love it when you wear them, you look so hot, but it's only for me, okay? Understood?"

Translation: "You'll wear what I want you to wear, and wear it when I say so."

- Directly or indirectly, they always make you think that there's someone out there who is better than you.

They want you to draw comparisons. It doesn't matter who they're comparing you to. It could be a friend, an ex, an actor, or an actress. They always do it in front of you. They'll always say nice things about that person, as if that person can do no wrong.

And to be clear, the problem isn't idolizing someone, the problem is hammering the point home to crush your partner.

Remember: You will never be enough for the wrong person.

This brings us to discuss the concept of the "phantom ex".

A phantom ex is the ex that your partner had before meeting you. But watch out, this is not just any ex-partner, this ex is perfect. In your partner's eyes, this ex did everything brilliantly: they were intelligent, patient, a good person, classy, hard-working … The person who they "felt the most" for, and who, for the rest of their lifetime, will probably remain their strongest connection. Or at least this is what you believe and how you perceive it. But actually, this is no more than a feeling and doesn't match the reality.

Some people, following a breakup, go from not valuing the person they were with at all to absolutely idolizing them: "She was the one who always understood me best, who put up with all my moods."

It is important to emphasize that this is purely a form of manipulation if the person who entertains this "phantom ex" communicates how perfect they were to their current partner. Not only that, but this phantom ex can also be used as a form of protest behavior to intentionally stoke jealousy in the other person (retroactive jealousy, something which I will talk about in the next chapter).

The opposite of having a "phantom ex" is a person who says, "All my exes were crazy."

This is a major *red flag*, watch out! What the person who thinks that "everyone in the world is crazy except for me" is really saying here is that the ex was actually totally normal. It's a line which logically demonstrates that, at the critical moment, this person twists things around to avoid taking any responsibility or blame.

Over the years, I have clearly seen that there are people who consciously manipulate others, and there are those who do it completely unwittingly. I have seen people simultaneously being both victims and perpetrators within a relationship. So, this isn't about good guys and bad guys, it's about understanding, observing, learning, and changing.

BENCHING

Benching is another form of emotional abuse which takes its name from the sporting practice of leaving a player "on the bench" (i.e. on the sidelines). So that you can understand it from the point of view of the person doing the "benching", it's about being insufficiently clear with someone, constantly being torn between showing interest and outright rejecting them; this is "benching" someone.

From the victim's point of view, from the moment you become someone's "plan B" or second choice, that person is benching you.

They're keeping you there, "on the bench", in case their plan A falls through. They're not interested in you for any other reason. They'll only seek your company to entertain themselves while they wait for their plan A. They'll talk to you now and again to keep stringing you along. Hedging their bets with you makes them feel safer, and you will have to settle for those breadcrumbs, unless you set boundaries.

So, if anyone has ever done this to you, they were failing to fulfil their affective responsibility, they were being dishonest, and they cared very little about how you felt.

If you find someone speaking to you occasionally, giving mixed signals, they don't spend much time with you, they disappear (ghosting), and reappear after a few days, without explanation, then I'm sorry to say, that person is not interested in you. They are keeping you benched.

GASLIGHTING

Gaslighting is another form of emotional abuse which is aimed at warping the other person's perception of reality and making them doubt their own sanity.

So that you can understand this from a behavioral perspective, from how it begins, and where it can lead, I'll tell you about my experience with Matt (not his real name).

Matt was a guy my age who I met one night while I was leaving a party. After that night, we talked for a bit on social media and went on a couple of dates. A few weeks after meeting him, he told me that he had fallen head over heels in love with me, and I, of course, believed him. Why would he lie to me? He also said that he had never met anyone like me, that I was beautiful and intelligent, and that, even though we hadn't known each other for very long, he felt sure that I was the love of his life.

We had lovely dates, we spoke every day, and the truth is that he made me feel so special that at no point could I ever have imagined what would transpire.

Time went on, and I lived my own life. I had my studies, my friends, and him. I started to see some inconsistencies in his behavior: he'd become less available than he was in the beginning, and I had the feeling that he was taking longer to reply to my messages. I got the sense that he was avoiding me, but I didn't want to dwell on it, and I carried on in the relationship as if nothing was wrong. After a few days, and after having seen that there was an endless supply of women interacting with him on social media, and that he was replying to them while ignoring me, I confronted him about what was going on. I told him that I felt there was some distance between us, and that I thought he was overlooking me in favor of focusing on other people. I approached it from a place of understanding, saying that I understood, and that if that was what he wanted, we could end our relationship with no hard feelings.

"Those girls are all friends with Jack's girlfriend. We went out with them together the other day and they added us all," Matt explained.

I, thinking that Matt loved me, and that we had something special together, dropped it and gave it no more thought. Meanwhile, Matt started showing less and less interest in me. Sometimes, he gave everything to the relationship, and I felt so much love, my cup was overflowing; yet on other occasions he completely ignored me, as if I didn't exist. Every time he paid me a little attention, I went out of my way for him; I tried to be the best girlfriend I could possibly be, so that, just in case he met someone else, he wouldn't notice them and would only want to be with me.

"Don't let me down, hey", he said, to make matters worse, implying that I shouldn't do anything to make him distrust me.

Given the circumstances, since there were days at a time when I didn't hear from him, my only option was to keep an eye on his social media. I know, very bad on my part (I'll explain why later on), but honestly, it was that or go crazy from the uncertainty.

"Hey Matt, it's been a few days and I haven't heard from you. Is everything alright?"

"Yeah, it's all good. I've just been really busy, but you know I love you tons babe, you're the love of my life."

And there I stayed, accepting these little crumbs of affection for a whole year. Until one day.

While I was in a local café, a girl who looked familiar stood in front of me and said:

"Hey, are you Matt's girlfriend?"

"Yes," I replied, rattled. Although I hadn't met her before, I knew who she was. I had seen her on Matt's social media sometimes.

"Great. Me too."

I don't know how I stayed standing. I couldn't believe what I was hearing.

I couldn't say anything, so she carried on.

"Look, I know it's fucked up, but I think Matt's been lying to both of us, and I think you should know the truth. Write down my Facebook username and password and log in. You have my full permission to read all the messages he's been sending me while he's been with you."

"Are you sure?" I mumbled, to a woman performing the most sisterly act that anyone has ever done for me in my entire life.

She took my hand and said firmly:

"Totally. It's only fair for both of us."

At the time, I didn't tell anyone what had happened. I still wasn't completely sure whether this was just some kind of joke in poor taste.

When I got home that afternoon, the first thing I did was get on the Internet from my computer. I was seized by a tremendous sense of anxiety the moment I saw the little boxes: Username … Password … waiting to be filled in. I could barely breathe. I was so scared of what I was about to find. How could he be capable of lying to me like this?

I typed in the login details that the girl had given me. And just like that, bingo, I was on her profile. "It cannot be true; it cannot be true . . . I kept thinking, over and over again. But with every passing moment, it was becoming more real. Something inside me wanted the login details to be fake.

I opened the private messages, and there lurked the conversation with Matt. My world crumbled.

I clicked on the conversation and began to read all the messages, one by one, from the start. Every word, like daggers, pierced me to the core.

And then, suddenly, I felt calm.

I don't know how or why my body suddenly decided not to suffer any more. It was probably the shock of the moment, because I don't remember much after that, but something inside me decided to draw a line under it. I was tired of suffering. I'd had enough pain. It was time to end it and let numbness take over. Nothing. That's what I felt. Nothing. Complete indifference.

It might seem paradoxical, but I think that, on discovering his betrayal, the pain was so intense that my brain decided to numb it.

All I could do until the following day was simply stare into the void while tying up loose ends. And, like some poor lost soul, I wandered from one side of the house to the other, consumed by my thoughts. How am I going to be able to tell him what I saw?

And so, as best I could, I started indirectly asking questions, testing the waters. He denied everything. He hadn't met anyone, he hadn't dated anyone, he didn't know who this girl was and, of course, she was following him on social media because she was probably obsessed with him.

So, I let him have it. I revealed everything. I even showed him screenshots of the messages. I had him cornered.

Do you think he had the decency to admit to what I had seen with my own eyes? Of course not.

The first thing he told me was that his identity had been stolen. In the face of my rising anger, he blurted out that it was this girl who was after him.

Just minutes later he confessed that I was right, he had talked to her, but he had only played along because she threatened to tell me if he didn't talk to her.

Then he played the loneliness card, saying that he felt all alone and that it was my fault.

And lastly, far from admitting the truth and apologizing, he tried to make out that he had simply been carried away by the situation, although, in reality, he loved me, and he acknowledged that he had a problem with his impulsiveness, and that I had to help him.

And, as unbelievable as it may seem, for an instant I hesitated. My God, how I wince whenever I think about this. In hindsight it seems so clear . . . But at that moment I doubted my own sanity. What if he really loved me and genuinely did have an impulse control problem that could be sorted out in therapy? In truth, I think that excuse would have been great if it weren't for the fact that the rest of the relationship, to be honest, was a complete mess. But at the time I hesitated. Of course I did. I was completely overwhelmed with memories of all those times when, according to him, my judgement "made no sense", because he loved me and he would never do that to me. I mean, not because he showed me love through his actions, but because he told me that he loved me with his words. It's ridiculous, I know, but when I was being manipulated, I didn't see it as clearly as I do now.

This all happened a long time ago, but I still remember parts of it as if it were yesterday.

I went back to talk to Angela. We'll call her that, because, honestly, this girl was like a guardian angel to me. She appeared out of nowhere and only left after saving me from continuing to live a lie.

"María, I also thought he loved me, and to tell you the truth, I knew you existed, but not because I knew you were his partner, only because I once saw a gift you gave him in his bedroom. When I asked about it, he said you were a friend who had become obsessed with him."

In that very moment, the scales fell from my eyes. Matt had used the same excuse with me to explain away the existence of other people in his life. We were all apparently crazy and obsessed with him.

Matt was lying to me. And, fair enough, you might say "Obviously! Couldn't you see it?" Well, no, actually. This manipulated and minimized person, even though the situation was more crystal clear than spring water, absolutely, categorically, didn't see it.

I never heard from Angela again. After talking, letting me see Matt for who he really was, and apologizing to each other, she vanished from my life.

Matt, on the other hand, did not give up. He continued to harass me and attempted to convince me that he loved me for several more months. At first, he got a response from me (it is hard to disengage), but I slowly became wise to his lies and manipulation tactics. And although, at the time, I didn't have the vocabulary to describe what he was doing to me, I now know that it was a wild form of gaslighting. I finally managed to let go of any desire to be with him.

Gaslighting can also take place in the form of emotional invalidation. Here are a few examples of things that someone might say to you if they were trying to invalidate your feelings.

OTHER EXAMPLES OF GASLIGHTING:

- Are you seriously crying about that?
- You're a bit "extra".
- That's nonsense.
- It's not that big of a deal.
- What a stupid thing to be worried about.
- Here we go again, you're getting worked up about everything.
- You are such a whiner.
- The one who needs therapy is you.
- You don't have to be like that.
- You are crazy.
- I lied to you because you get angry about the slightest thing.

The consequences for the victim, as you've already seen, are that, during conflicts, they suffer the indignity of having their feelings minimized and painted as something embarrassing, to be ashamed of.

Invalidating emotions is something that many people do without even realizing it, probably because they grew up in an environment where feelings were typically invalidated. Usually, the ways we've learned to relate to others and to ourselves throughout our lives, especially during childhood, are what will later be reflected in our relationships with our partners.

Let me tell you about Ross and Jamie, a couple I once saw in consultation who, although they didn't have a dependent bond, and their relationship overall was fairly healthy, we discovered in session that Jamie invalidated Ross totally unwittingly. Delving into Jamie's background, I discovered that for his whole life he had also received the type of comments listed above, coming from his family, so it was something that he had normalized. Ross, on the other hand, had easily recognized that such comments were not normal and they did not sit well with him. In the absence of a dependent relationship or toxic dynamics, as I mentioned earlier (in relationships with dependency issues and toxicity, going to therapy as a couple is not recommended, since the probability of success is zero), we were able to carry out a couple's intervention.

"Well, what am I meant to say to him, María?" Jamie was asking in the session, "If it's true that I think he really does get worked up over silly little things!"

"I hear what you're saying, but for him, in the moment, it is not silly. If he thought it didn't matter, he wouldn't be bringing it up with you. What will end up happening with this dynamic is that Ross will stop telling you how he feels, and you will long to see the real him more and more."

"That's true, he is telling me less and less, and it seems like each time I'm the one who has to go and figure out what he's thinking. Why doesn't he tell me stuff? I'm always having to go around him, guessing."

"Well, Jamie, this is a consequence of what I've been talking about. If he tells you things and you answer him the way you have been doing, you make him feel invalidated. It is like receiving a punishment."

"Do you really think so?"

"Absolutely. How would you like it if you were sitting here telling me about a problem you're having, and I just turned around and called you a whiner?"

"No, of course I wouldn't like that, you are my psychologist."

"Well, he is your husband." After a beat of silence, where Jamie seemed pensive, I pressed on: "Why don't you try it?" Jaime sighed and, after a few more seconds of silent reflection, he slowly nodded.

"I'll give it a go," he agreed. "Now that you've told me, I will."

After several months of hard work in our sessions and at home, Ross and Jamie changed their whole patterns of behavior and communication. Jamie stopped invalidating Ross's emotions and Ross, feeling that Jamie was no longer judging him quite so harshly, began to trust and communicate better with his partner, something that he had also been longing for.

One of the guidelines I gave Jamie was to practice different ways of giving his partner feedback, without feeling the need to invalidate him. So here are some examples for you to practice too if you wish:

- I may not share your feelings on this, but I respect that you feel that way.
- I will make an effort to understand where you're coming from.
- I'm sorry you are upset.
- Is there anything I can do to help?
- Cry if you need to.

- How do you feel?
- I understand that this is important to you.
- It is normal to feel this way.
- I am listening.
- I don't know what to tell you right now because I kind of need time to process this. I'll make a cup of tea and if you want you can tell me more in depth.
- Give them a hug and sit next to them without saying a word.

Of course, it's not often that we see cases like Ross and Jamie's. What we usually see in terms of gaslighting or emotional invalidation are, unfortunately, cases which play out more like what happened with me and Matt.

♥ 7 ♥

JEALOUSY

I imagine that, by this point, we all understand perfectly well that jealousy is not love. So, if you've ever had someone try to sell you a lie by telling you this rubbish, it was most likely someone with beliefs about love and relationships worthy of the Middle Ages. Although I don't blame them either. From the TV shows on our screens, to the success of books which later got turned into films such as *Twilight*, *Fifty Shades of Grey* and *After*, I blame these. Rather than being love stories, they are actually stories of romanticized harassment, abuse, and emotional dependence. Things like these normalize the concept of "possession" as love (and may whoever is without sin, cast the first stone).

But, just as disappointment is not joy, and anger is not disgust; jealousy is not love. Love and jealousy are two completely different concepts. They don't imply anything more transcendental than simply being feelings. Therefore, the association between jealousy and love makes no logical sense, but as a society we still make this link thanks to certain deep-rooted macho beliefs embedded within our culture that equate love with possession.

I have met both those who claim that jealousy is undoubtedly a bad thing, as well as those who unequivocally believe that being jealous is positive. So, who has it right? Neither. Jealousy is neither good nor bad, it is simply an emotion. There are no good or bad emotions. Everything depends on how they are handled. If managing an emotion involves controlling a partner, then what is bad (or rather, dysfunctional) is the management itself, the association made between jealousy and love, and the quality of the bond, or the way the person has learned to relate to the partner, but the emotion itself is not wrong.

Jealousy occurs as a response to a situation that is perceived as a threat, but it is a secondary emotion, resulting from a mixture of anger and fear (both primary emotions), which means that, when we feel jealousy, we are simultaneously feeling fear and anger. In terms of attachment (we will look at this term in more detail later), our brains are more basic than a cardboard box, so any stimulus that we perceive as a potential threat, i.e., something that increases the likelihood of a possible "loss" of the partner, will trigger all those emotions. This process, up to this point, is totally normal and can happen to anyone, so you mustn't feel ashamed if you or your partner have ever succumbed to jealousy. However, it is one thing to feel jealous, and quite another to get carried away by it and let it affect your conduct or behavior.

When working on managing jealousy, we look at all the things which might be considered a threat, how they are perceived and interpreted, and aim to learn better coping skills for channeling and handling that emotion differently, so that the resulting behavior doesn't cause suffering to the people involved, nor become dysfunctional within the relationship. What we want to achieve with this is to avoid the slippery slope into controlling behavior towards their partner and, consequently, suffering on both sides.

For example, if your partner is exchanging messages with a friend but never mentions it to you, however you happen to find out anyway because one day, by chance, you see a notification, well, hey, maybe don't immediately leap to conclusions and make a big deal out of it. First, calm down, and work out what's actually going on. And then, of course, you can bring it up with your partner, because, and

I can't stress this enough, bringing your partner on board in these situations is extremely important. If there is already a boatload of accusations flying between the two of you, you can see how that leaves very little room for cooperation in managing the situation and handling this jealousy, right? Let's do things right.

To know how to handle emotions, it is essential to understand the main purpose of each emotion itself. Remember that jealousy comes from triggering anger and fear, two very nice emotions that always go hand in hand. Didn't you know? When one is triggered, the other is triggered too. Always. Take a look next time and you will see. (This, in case you are interested in going deeper, is due to a biological process that Manuel Hernández Pacheco explains very well in his book *Attachment and Psychopathology: Anxiety and its Origin.)* Therefore, if we can understand what purpose is served by the emotions of fear and anger, then we can also understand the purpose of jealousy.

We already know this because I just told you: our brain is having an instinctive response to a potential threat. But the idea of what constitutes a "potential threat" should be taken with a pinch of salt because, as we all know, everyone sees and processes things differently. And no, this is not about "being wrong in the head", this, I promise you, happens to all of us, but we must be self-aware and rational about it.

Let's take a look at a practical example of how processing jealousy works.

WHAT DO YOU SEE HERE?

YOU HAVE THREE SECONDS TO GIVE YOUR ANSWER.

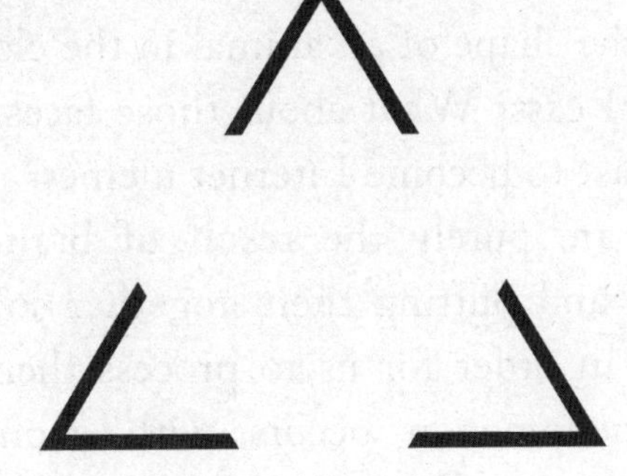

THREE. TWO. ONE.

A TRIANGLE, RIGHT? AHA. WHAT IF I SHOW YOU THIS?

IS IT ANOTHER TRIANGLE? IS IT A PART OF THE FIRST TRIANGLE?

AND THIS?

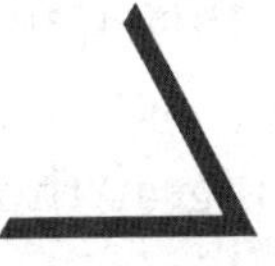

AND THIS?

Well, actually, what I'm showing you is simply six lines placed in such a way that your brain interprets them as a particular shape. Our brains are hardwired to do this. Have you ever seen the shape of an animal in the clouds? Or faces on the fronts of cars? What about those faces which appear on pieces of toast to become Internet memes?

Well, these are purely the result of brain mechanisms finding shapes and putting them together so that they are familiar to us, in order for us to process them more easily. When the phenomenon occurs with geometric shapes, we call it pareidolia. This way of processing things is an evolutionary trait that we developed to protect ourselves from possible dangers. The faster we can process things, the quicker we can protect ourselves. We can't process something fast if we have to look at it bit by bit; it's better to quickly smash it all together in our heads and assign it to something familiar, to make the job easier. Thousands of years ago, this is what our ancestors were doing. They needed to be able to see the faces of any possible predators in among the trees or rocks. Nowadays we don't have to deal with predators, but the truth is that those residual traits and the principles of Gestalt psychology could explain this quick and easy processing, which is slowly disappearing. Let's call it cognitive shorthand.

So, while you were looking at those diagrams, your brain was probably saying something like this: "Six lines, placed at 60-degree angles, in such a way as they remind me of a triangle? It must be a triangle then. I will fill in the missing lines myself."

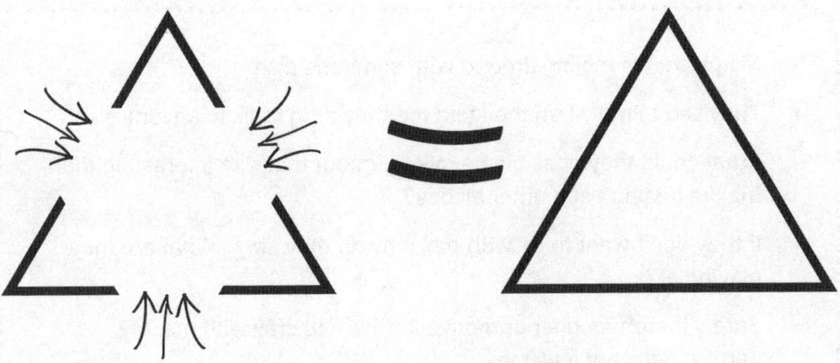

And that's what happens: our brain "completes" the gaps in the picture with the information it already knows.

This cognitive phenomenon, when it occurs with thoughts, is called confirmation bias, also known as the tendency to prefer, seek, interpret, and remember information which confirms one's own previous beliefs, ignoring other possible alternatives.

Let's return to the previous example.

Your partner is exchanging messages with a friend but never mentions it to you; however, you happen to find out anyway because one day, by chance, you see a notification. What would you think about this?

If you've never experienced infidelity and this is the first time it's happened to you, your warning system probably won't even be activated, but what if it is? You might end up thinking things such as:

- My partner is fooling around with someone else.
- They lied to me when they told me they didn't talk to anyone else.
- What could they possibly be talking about that's so interesting that they're texting each other all day?
- If they don't want to be with me, why do they stay? What are they playing at?
- Surely there's an ulterior motive for them to stay with me. My partner does not love me.
- I knew I could never trust anyone.
- It is better to be alone than in bad company.
- They'll see, I'm going to give them a piece of my mind.
- I'm going to leave them – they can go to hell.

It is true that, as we have previously seen, our own past has a significant influence on how we process things (i.e. when the brain fills in the missing information, it uses things that it already knows or is familiar with), but when the brain's alarm system is activated, it is activated, and there is no stopping it, unless you pay careful attention to what is going on inside your head.

If the fuse is lit, Rome will burn, unless you are aware that your brain is currently in survival mode and is only seeking to "defend" you from a danger that, as you already know, it probably invented, just like the imaginary sides of the triangle, thanks to those evolutionary traits.

"But what if it's true, María? What if she is really fooling around with someone else and she's hiding it from me?" asked Patricia, a patient I was working with to help manage her jealousy in her relationship with Monica. Despite never having given Patricia any cause for concern, Monica was paying for the mistakes of people in her partner's past. Patricia had already experienced infidelity in a previous relationship.

"And what if it's not?" I answered. "It's an equal probability. And a good reason not to make unilateral decisions. Why not discuss it with her calmly?"

"But she'll probably feel bad about me doubting her."

"You may decide not to talk to her for fear of upsetting her, but that won't stop it from going round in circles in your head."

"Yeah ... and in the end that is worse, because I am struggling with the weight of my own thoughts ..."

"And you will probably end up having the conversation anyway, but it'll be in a bad way because you'll have been brooding on it for some time. We already know how toxic it is to have an explosive drama like this in a relationship. Do you think that discussing your fears could help you to be calmer?" I asked, giving her time to reflect.

After a few seconds of silence, Patricia spoke up.

"Yes ... I think that's what I'll do."

"I think that's a good idea. In any case, consider this: if she is offended by you opening up to her and sharing your emotions and concerns, then it says more about her than it does about you."

"At the end of the day, whatever she says, it will be a good thing for me. You're right. I don't think I would be offended if my partner opened up to me like that." Patricia paused, and after a bit more reflection, she said "Hey, if she's offended because I say I'm suspicious of her, what should I say then?"

"You can explain to her everything you've learned about jealousy in this session, can't you?"

Patricia left the consultation with fresh determination to discuss the situation with Monica. Her partner not only understood her and offered support, but also wanted to negotiate with Patricia so that, whenever she felt that way, she would tell her, and Monica would do everything possible to help her manage her emotions. And that's how important it is to have both partners on board. They can provide fundamental support, even when the problem is between the couple.

WHY IS IT IMPORTANT TO HELP THE PARTNER MANAGE THEIR EMOTIONS?

People need to feel that their surroundings provide safety and stability. Life is not always easy, and we often experience negative events, problems, unforeseen circumstances, critical moments, and bad days. In the face of this, it is both important and necessary that anybody in turmoil finds their partner to be a notable source of support.

Given that a partner is one of your nearest and dearest, it is their responsibility to provide emotional stability when the other person needs it. Although they may not exactly understand or share the same perspective as the person in emotional distress, it is vitally important for the partner to listen, ask questions, and show that they are present. This is an affective responsibility.

The person in emotional distress must manage their feelings on an individual level. However, if the partner is not there to provide that baseline stability and support, then individual management is like fighting against the tide.

Demonstrating emotional stability does not mean solving problems or taking responsibility for the emotion, it simply means accompanying and, via verbal or non-verbal communication, sending a reassuring message: "Hey, I'm here, everything will be okay, don't worry. Let me give you a hug."

If, when faced with individual emotional discomfort, the partner acts distant, without taking responsibility for their part in what's causing it, then the one who's suffering will continue to suffer even more. This is known as individualism in relationships. Spoiler alert: It doesn't work. It creates an ambivalent environment and a certain rivalry with the partner.

HERE'S AN EXAMPLE OF WHAT WORKS WHEN DEALING WITH JEALOUSY:

WHAT WORKS:

"How are you feeling? Why do you feel that way? I am listening. You know I love you and would never do that to you. Also, whenever you feel that way, please let me know and we'll talk about it."

WHAT DOESN'T WORK:

"If it's my partner who is jealous and I know I'm not doing anything wrong, let them deal with it."

Let's look at some other examples of how to support someone to handle their emotions. Let's imagine that something has happened and your partner is all riled up about it.

WHAT WORKS:

"What's up? I might not be able to understand it, but it seems to be important to you. Is there anything I can do to help make you feel better?"

WHAT DOESN'T WORK:

"What a load of rubbish. You're getting worked up over this? There are more important things."

Now imagine that you had an argument with your partner over something you did and it made them feel bad, even though you didn't mean to.

WHAT WORKS:

"That wasn't my intention. Still, I'm sorry I made you feel bad."

WHAT DOESN'T WORK:

"I don't think it's right for you to be angry about this, I didn't do what you're accusing me of. You've hurt me too in the past, and I didn't react like that."

In a moment I'll show you a conversation where jealousy could not have been handled any worse. In it, the discussion ends in a fight because the topic is approached with an aggressive communication style and a bad attitude; and what's more, it is replete with all kinds of emotional invalidation.

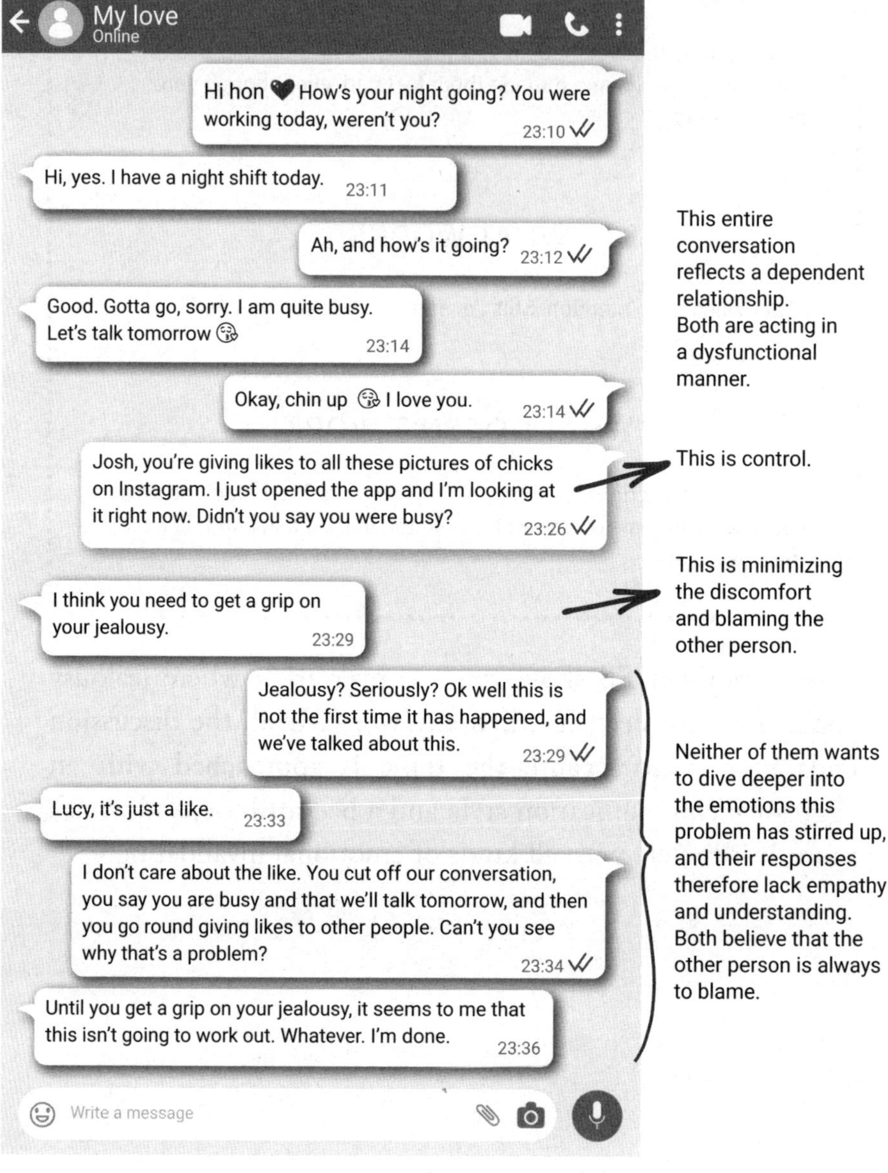
My love
Online
Hi hon ❤ How's your night going? You were working today, weren't you? 23:10
Hi, yes. I have a night shift today. 23:11
Ah, and how's it going? 23:12
Good. Gotta go, sorry. I am quite busy. Let's talk tomorrow 😘 23:14
Okay, chin up 😘 I love you. 23:14
Josh, you're giving likes to all these pictures of chicks on Instagram. I just opened the app and I'm looking at it right now. Didn't you say you were busy? 23:26
I think you need to get a grip on your jealousy. 23:29
Jealousy? Seriously? Ok well this is not the first time it has happened, and we've talked about this. 23:29
Lucy, it's just a like. 23:33
I don't care about the like. You cut off our conversation, you say you are busy and that we'll talk tomorrow, and then you go round giving likes to other people. Can't you see why that's a problem? 23:34
Until you get a grip on your jealousy, it seems to me that this isn't going to work out. Whatever. I'm done. 23:36
Write a message
This entire conversation reflects a dependent relationship. Both are acting in a dysfunctional manner.
This is control.
This is minimizing the discomfort and blaming the other person.
Neither of them wants to dive deeper into the emotions this problem has stirred up, and their responses therefore lack empathy and understanding. Both believe that the other person is always to blame.

Now, I want to show you a different scenario, handled in a more functional way.

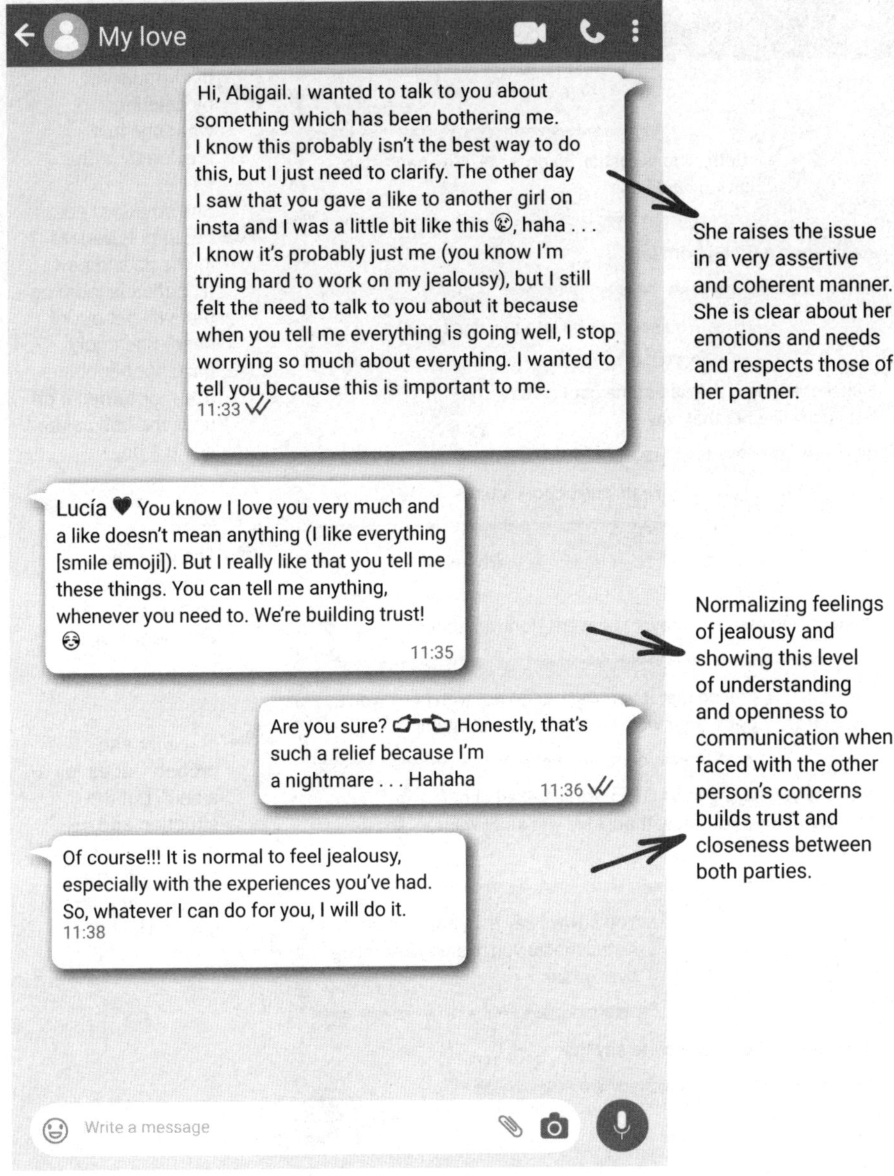

Now, let's look at how the same situation could be badly managed and well managed.

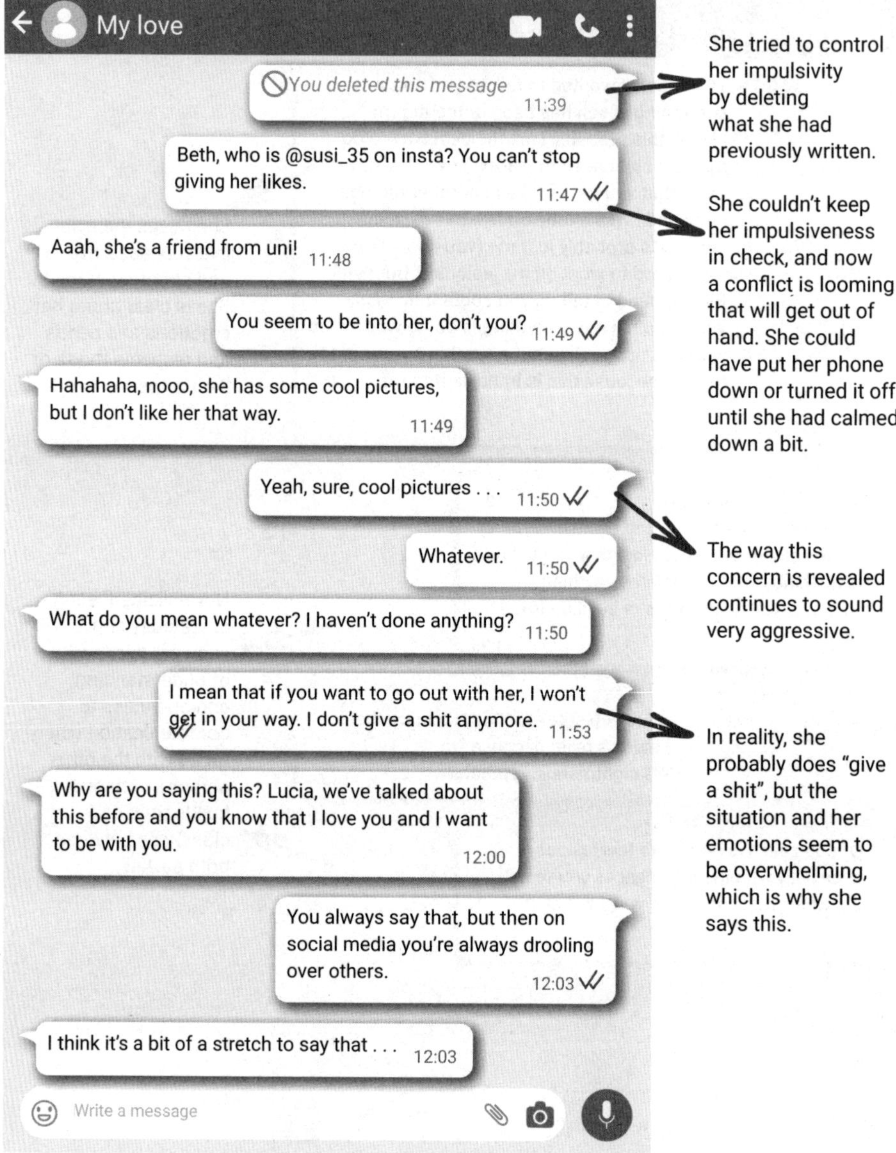

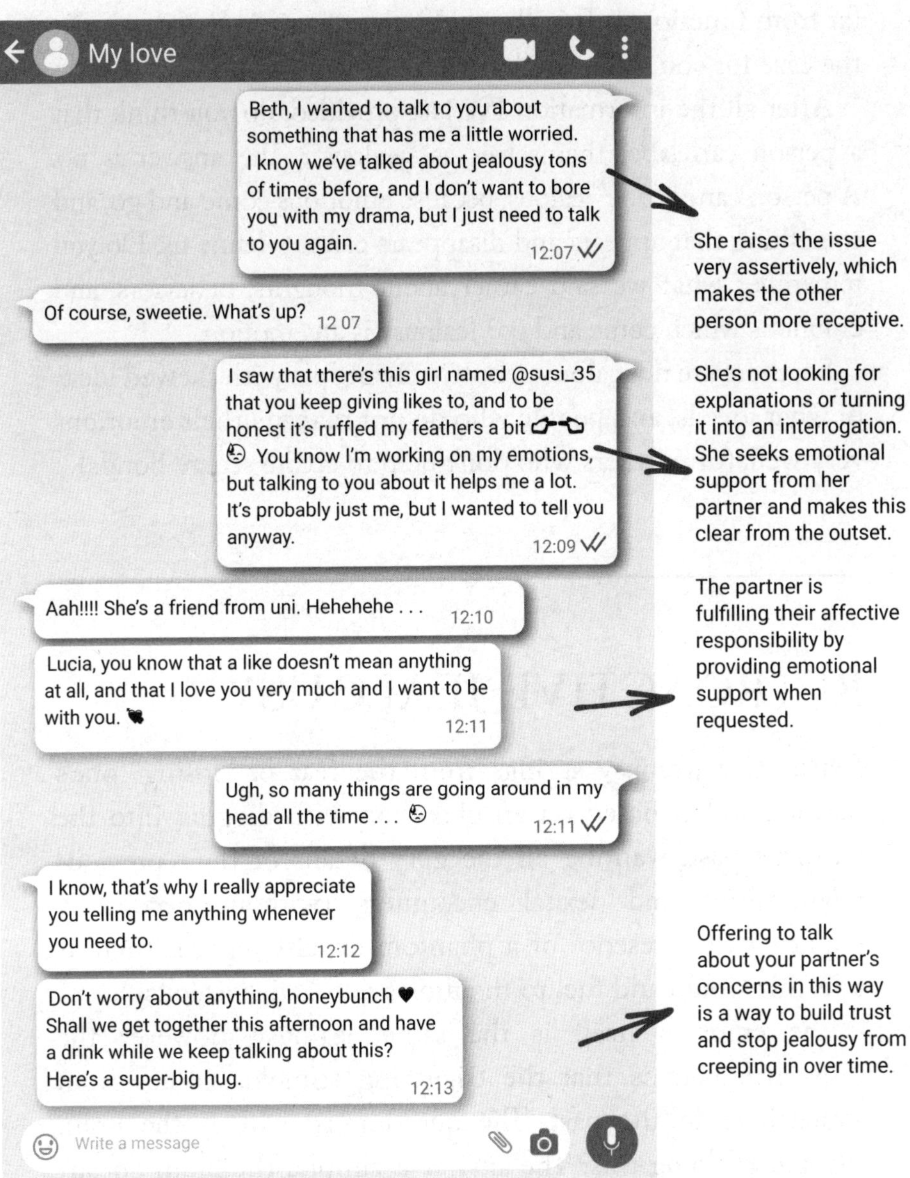

There's a difference, isn't there? If finding a functional way to handle jealousy in a relationship seems like an impossible dream to you, then I'm afraid to say it, but your relationship is far from functional. This should be the norm. And if that's not the case for you, then you have a lot of work to do.

After all the information I've just provided, do you think that a person can label themselves as "jealous"? The answer is no. A person cannot "be" jealous, because emotions come and go, and something that appears and disappears cannot define us. Do you remember what we said earlier about thoughts, behaviors, and emotions which come and go? Jealousy is an emotion.

So, there are no jealous people, only people with skewed ideas of what love is, and people who do not manage their emotions very well, (or partners who don't help to create secure bonds).

RETROACTIVE JEALOUSY

Retroactive jealousy springs from the fear of "losing" one's partner, and is based on an obsession with digging into the partner's past, wanting all the gory details of their previous relationships and sexual encounters (without necessarily requiring the presence of a phantom ex, although, if there is one, this would add fuel to the fire of retroactive jealousy).

The emotion itself is the same, jealousy, however the difference here is that the triggering stimulus comes from somewhere in the past. The question is: why is the brain capable of doing this? The answer is simple. The brain doesn't understand time. To the brain, there is no difference between a memory from three years ago, and a situation that you fear will happen in four days' time. It cannot distinguish between these two. As soon as a stimulus (in this case a thought) is given, the brain processes it as if it were happening right now. In other words, the brain only understands the present tense.

It also has no idea what is real or not real, objectively speaking. If you have something in front of you, no matter how surreal it may be, for the brain it is real. There is no way around it. Afraid of making a fool of yourself in your first business meeting? Don't worry, your brain will take care of it, processing the fear as if it were actually happening to you right now. What do you notice? Anxiety, obviously. For the brain, the thing you're dreading is happening right now, at this exact moment, and it reacts with an anxiety response. Just try it out, think of something that makes you feel the emotion you want to induce, and you will see how after a few seconds or minutes you begin to feel that emotion. The mind is incredibly powerful.

It's exactly the same with jealousy. The more you flood your mind with thoughts of past or current suspicions, the more "present" they feel to you, and the more you obsess over them.

What are the symptoms of someone in the throes of retroactive jealousy?

- They want to know every detail of the current partner's past relationships.
- It seems that no amount of detail is ever enough, they always want to know more. They are particularly obsessed with knowing what the previous partner looked like physically, what they were like as a person, how they treated the current partner, or how they made the current partner feel.

- They check the partner's mobile phone, calendar, emails, social media, etc. for more information. The intention behind checking for all of these "potential dangers" is actually to prove that everything is okay. In this scenario, "everything being okay" would mean checking to see that no one has tried getting in touch with the partner, as well as finding out what the partner's life was like with their ex-partners, and wanting to know all kinds of details, even the ones which might be hurtful.
- They need to feel that they are somehow "more important" and "better" than these past partners.
- They tend to demand explanations from the partner about what they did in the past.
- They constantly criticize the partner for things that they did in the past with another person or people.

A very curious thing about this type of jealousy and checking behaviors is that they are directly linked. Watch out, because if we let ourselves get carried away, we can find ourselves engaging in a set of very toxic behaviors indeed.

When we get into a habit of reducing discomfort by resorting to these types of checks, what we are actually doing is taking the discomfort caused by uncertainty and jealousy and linking it to the idea that it can be reduced by checking that everything is still fine. The problem is that this dynamic is addictive. Checking that everything is okay might, at first, calm us down for a few days, but if we become accustomed to compulsively checking, it will calm us down less and less each time, to the point where doing these checks barely calms us down even for a few seconds. It is not a good tool for managing emotions.

What thoughts can trigger retroactive jealousy?

- "My partner doesn't give me the attention I deserve."

Be careful, because this thought could spring from one of two things, either your expectations of what your partner should be doing in the relationship are too high, or it could be that your partner genuinely isn't meeting your needs in the relationship.

To get ahead of these doubts, I always recommend writing a list of what you consider to be the "bare minimum" in a relationship. What are the basics you require in order to feel that your partner is meeting your needs?

The difference between "bare minimum requirements", and straightforward "requirements" is that the list of bare minimums should be fundamental things that the person in question must weigh up, deciding whether or not these things are strictly necessary for the relationship to feel fulfilling. The aspects we need to be thinking about in order to create this list should be along the lines of:

- Communication.
- Spending time together.
- Affection.
- Sex and intimacy.
- Parenting (if there are any children).
- Philosophies about life together.
- Shared life goals.

So here is an example of what my list of minimum requirements would look like:

- Communication. I especially need to talk things through when something happens to us.
- Respect. To me, this means never raising our voices (and if we do, knowing how to stop and apologize), never insulting each other, and taking the things that might upset the other person into consideration.
- Empathy. Taking others' feelings into account.
- Knowing that you can count on one another.
- Feeling at peace with him by my side.
- Spending quality time together (especially at weekends).
- Speaking every day, whether by messages, phone, or in person.
- Feeling that my partner will be there through thick and thin. Feeling that he is there for me.

Now it's your turn.
My list of minimum requirements:

____

____

____

____

____

____

____

____

____

- "This has happened to me before."

This is a commonly recurring thought among those who have had past negative experiences and who now find themselves succumbing to retroactive jealousy.

- "My partner is cheating on me."

Then we have the typical phrases which looped back into all these thoughts (usually very unhelpfully).

There are three in particular that I have always taken issue with:

- "There's no smoke without fire."
- "Think the worst and you won't be far wrong."
- "Even a broken clock is right twice a day." My best friend told me this one.

When I suspected that I was with someone who wasn't treating me the way I thought they should, combined with unusual behavior, such as not responding to my messages, or avoiding meeting up with me, one of those phrases always rang loudly in my head.

Even worse, I seemed to attribute some sort of mystical universal truth to these words. Whenever they sprang to mind, I discovered infidelity or found evidence that, indeed, my partner at the time did not love me. And, so, in my mind they became linked to feelings and to the behaviors of the men I was with. They always rang true. "Think the worst and you won't be far wrong" and I did, I thought the worst, and indeed I wasn't wrong. But, what was the problem, exactly?

Aren't these sayings known to be unhelpful? Do they excuse my partner's infidelity? Of course not. Although I do admit that many times, even though I felt absolutely sure of my findings, I was still wrong for obvious reasons. My thoughts were most likely the result of me processing things based on what I had learned from past experiences.

On other occasions, what happened to me was a self-fulfilling prophecy. This is when something a person thinks ends up happening because their actions, influenced by their ideas, also end up influencing the outcome. In my case: I was scared that my partner would leave me for someone else, or stop loving me, so to prevent my fears from becoming reality, I showed an excessive interest in him. For example, questioning him in a very aggressive manner (on the assumption that he had been unfaithful), which overwhelmed my partner at the time and led him to distance himself from me.

Needless to say, although a self-fulfilling prophecy may occur, it is not a universal explanation for why couples drift apart when jealousy is at play.

However, with all this water under the bridge, there was something else making things worse, if that were possible, but I couldn't see it until much later, when I started working on myself.

Over time, as you have seen, I realized that I had developed almost a superstition about those sayings, and I thought that, surely, I was not the first and wouldn't be the last person to do so. I realized that most of the time (at least enough to reinforce my superstition), it wasn't about my feelings or suspicions, nor was it about whether the actual phrases crossed my mind or not; at the end of the day, it was about who I was with, and the type of men I tended to go for. When you are with someone who is blowing hot and cold, no traditional saying is going to sweep away your doubts; any misgivings that you feel should be cleared up right away, from the very start. You'll save yourself a lot of trouble. I will go into more detail on the "profile" of a person who does this, later on.

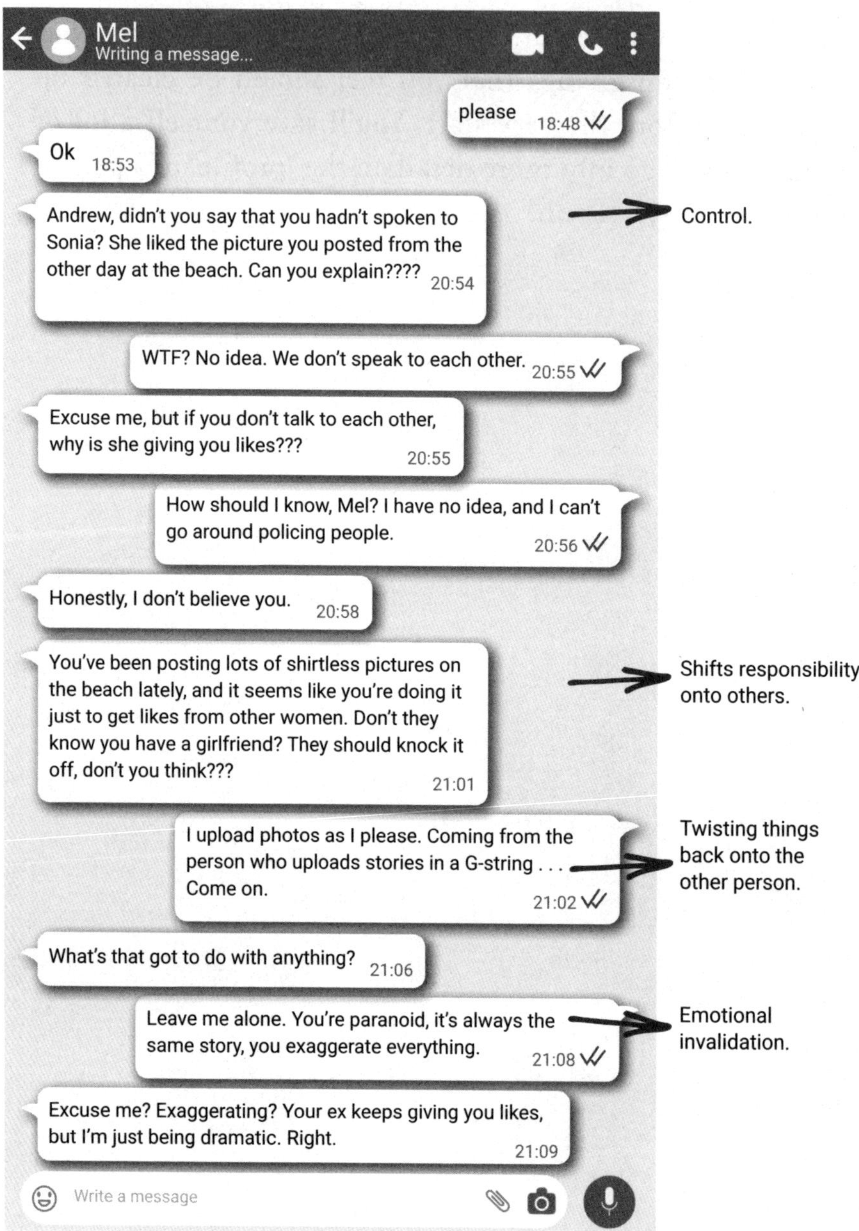
Mel
Writing a message...
please 18:48
Ok 18:53
Andrew, didn't you say that you hadn't spoken to Sonia? She liked the picture you posted from the other day at the beach. Can you explain???? 20:54
Control.
WTF? No idea. We don't speak to each other. 20:55
Excuse me, but if you don't talk to each other, why is she giving you likes??? 20:55
How should I know, Mel? I have no idea, and I can't go around policing people. 20:56
Honestly, I don't believe you. 20:58
You've been posting lots of shirtless pictures on the beach lately, and it seems like you're doing it just to get likes from other women. Don't they know you have a girlfriend? They should knock it off, don't you think??? 21:01
Shifts responsibility onto others.
I upload photos as I please. Coming from the person who uploads stories in a G-string . . . Come on. 21:02
Twisting things back onto the other person.
What's that got to do with anything? 21:06
Leave me alone. You're paranoid, it's always the same story, you exaggerate everything. 21:08
Emotional invalidation.
Excuse me? Exaggerating? Your ex keeps giving you likes, but I'm just being dramatic. Right. 21:09
Write a message

How to work on retroactive jealousy:

- Have an assertive conversation with your partner about the problems you are having with trying to manage this emotion.
- Put yourself in your partner's shoes (practice empathy).
- Try using physical relaxation and meditation techniques to calm your impulses around these police-like interrogations and checks.
- Remember that everyone, including you, has a past.
- Reflect on your thoughts.
- Seek professional help.

When you feel jealous, remember this:

♥ 8 ♥

THE PROFILE OF A NARCISSIST VERSUS THE PROFILE OF AN EMPATH

No, this is not a war, and they are not on opposing sides, although they might as well be.

As we saw in previous chapters, in almost all dependent relationships we see that, between the people involved, there is a marked imbalance between their roles; one almost always maintains a dominant attitude while the other is submissive.

The problem with these attitudes is that they correspond to personality profiles which have a fatal attraction to one another: narcissistic profiles and empathic profiles; polar opposites that attract to form the most toxic combination we can possibly see in a romantic relationship.

PEOPLE WITH A NARCISSISTIC PERSONALITY PROFILE:

- Need the adulation of others to strengthen their self-esteem.
- Need to be liked.
- Need to have another person at their "service" or waiting on them.
- Show a "false" version of themselves at first to attract others.
- Are very prone to ghosting.
- Often resort to manipulation tactics.
- Will make the other person feel guilty, even if the narcissist is the one who made the mistake.
- Never acknowledge their mistakes, and if they do, they will always find a way to shift some of the responsibility onto others.
- When presented with other solutions, they focus on how many times they have tried to do things that same way, but it didn't work out due to factors beyond their control (nothing is ever their fault).
- You may never become part of their social circle (friends, family, etc.).

- They are very charming to others. Perfect. There are two sides to them. Outwardly, they show their best side, they appear kind, friendly, and charismatic. Behind closed doors, in private, they can be very different.
- They often play a game of "punishment and repentance", where the other person is bound to respect their rules, or suffer the consequence of being completely trampled and overridden. In turn, the victim often has low self-esteem which makes it difficult to walk away.
- They are highly likely to idealize their partners when they are no longer together (the phantom ex).
- They keep coming back and attempt to "win over" the other person by doing things that they know the other person likes: saying nice things, doing something "right", etc.
- If the empathic person is aware that their emotional needs, dreams, and desires are also important, and communicates this, the narcissistic person will label them "selfish".
- They play the victim as a manipulation tactic.

TYPICAL THINGS THAT PEOPLE WITH A NARCISSISTIC PERSONALITY PROFILE MIGHT SAY INCLUDE:

"I know I'm not perfect. I want to change."

FOR THE PURPOSES OF CLARITY:

- **Victim:** A person who suffers physical or emotional harm from another.
- **Victim mentality:** A person who tends to perceive themself as a victim.
- **Manipulative victim mentality:** A manipulation and emotional abuse strategy whereby the person perceives themself to be the victim and makes this known to others, judging them all responsible for their suffering.

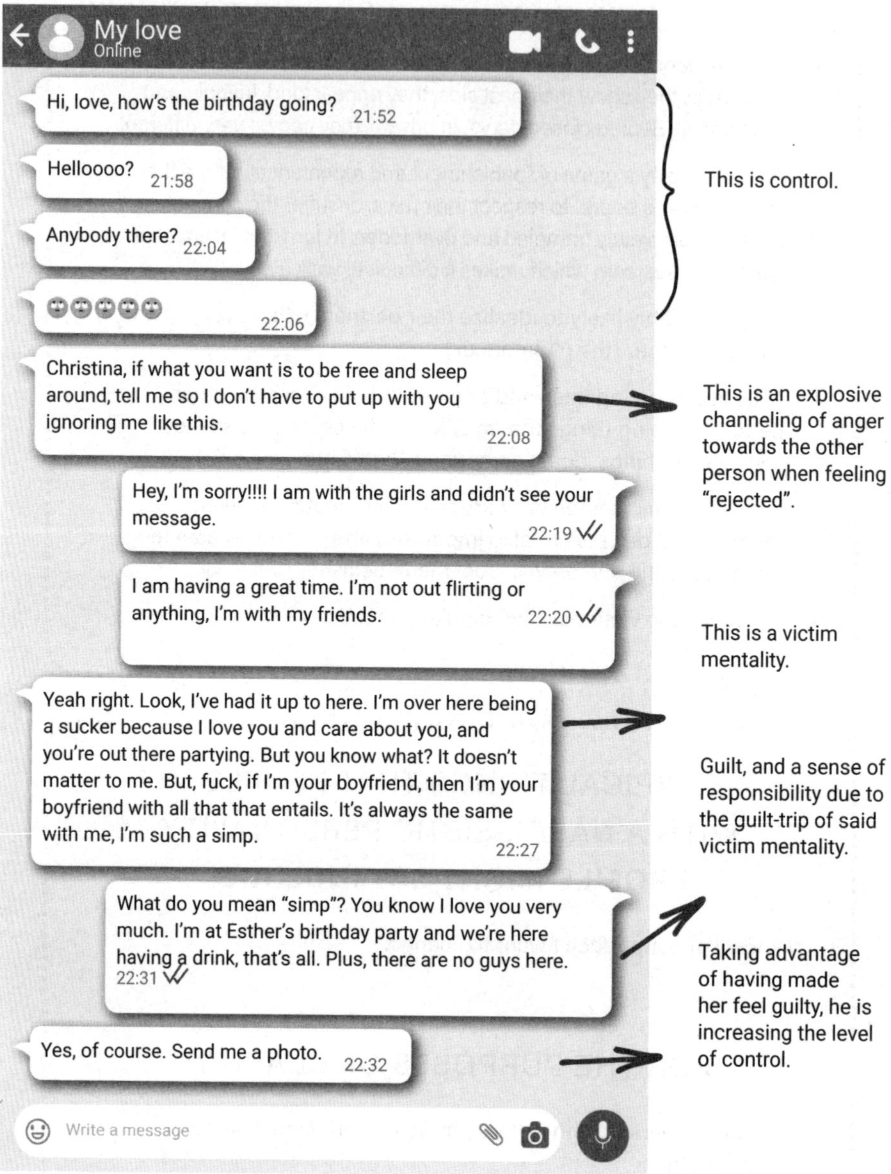
My love
Online
Hi, love, how's the birthday going? 21:52
Helloooo? 21:58
Anybody there? 22:04
22:06
Christina, if what you want is to be free and sleep around, tell me so I don't have to put up with you ignoring me like this. 22:08
Hey, I'm sorry!!!! I am with the girls and didn't see your message. 22:19
I am having a great time. I'm not out flirting or anything, I'm with my friends. 22:20
Yeah right. Look, I've had it up to here. I'm over here being a sucker because I love you and care about you, and you're out there partying. But you know what? It doesn't matter to me. But, fuck, if I'm your boyfriend, then I'm your boyfriend with all that that entails. It's always the same with me, I'm such a simp. 22:27
What do you mean "simp"? You know I love you very much. I'm at Esther's birthday party and we're here having a drink, that's all. Plus, there are no guys here. 22:31
Yes, of course. Send me a photo. 22:32
Write a message
This is control.
This is an explosive channeling of anger towards the other person when feeling "rejected".
This is a victim mentality.
Guilt, and a sense of responsibility due to the guilt-trip of said victim mentality.
Taking advantage of having made her feel guilty, he is increasing the level of control.

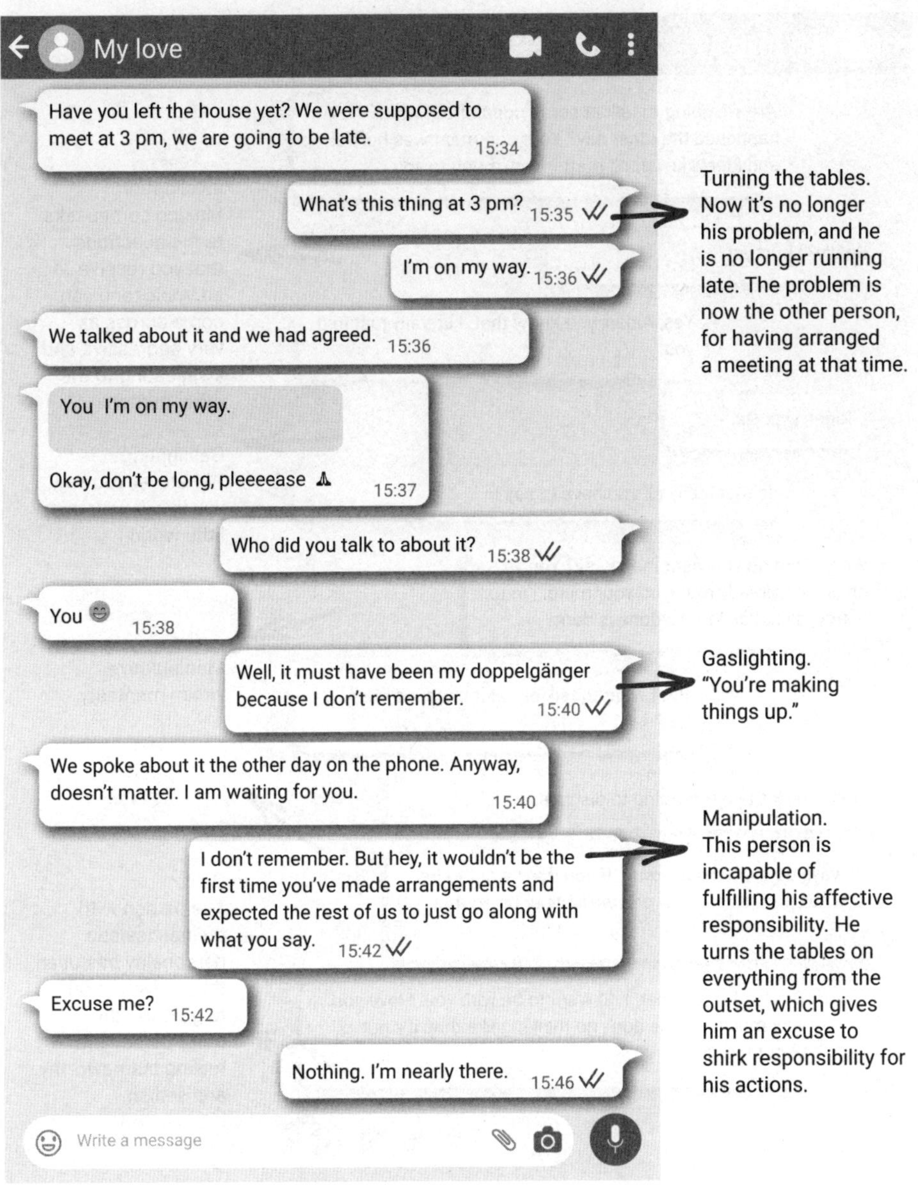
My love
Have you left the house yet? We were supposed to meet at 3 pm, we are going to be late. 15:34
What's this thing at 3 pm? 15:35
Turning the tables. Now it's no longer his problem, and he is no longer running late. The problem is now the other person, for having arranged a meeting at that time.
I'm on my way. 15:36
We talked about it and we had agreed. 15:36
You I'm on my way.
Okay, don't be long, pleeeease 15:37
Who did you talk to about it? 15:38
You 15:38
Well, it must have been my doppelgänger because I don't remember. 15:40
Gaslighting. "You're making things up."
We spoke about it the other day on the phone. Anyway, doesn't matter. I am waiting for you. 15:40
I don't remember. But hey, it wouldn't be the first time you've made arrangements and expected the rest of us to just go along with what you say. 15:42
Manipulation. This person is incapable of fulfilling his affective responsibility. He turns the tables on everything from the outset, which gives him an excuse to shirk responsibility for his actions.
Excuse me? 15:42
Nothing. I'm nearly there. 15:46
Write a message

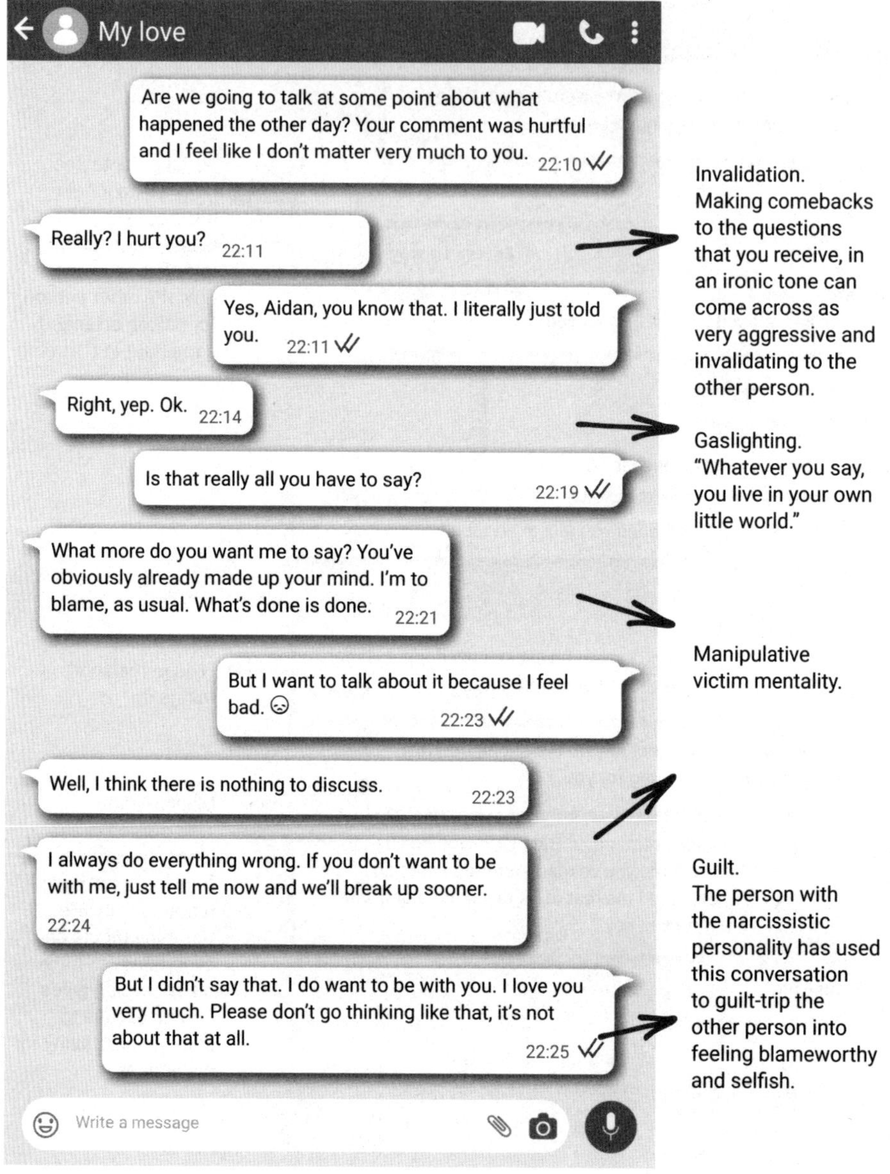
My love
Are we going to talk at some point about what happened the other day? Your comment was hurtful and I feel like I don't matter very much to you. 22:10
Really? I hurt you? 22:11
Yes, Aidan, you know that. I literally just told you. 22:11
Right, yep. Ok. 22:14
Is that really all you have to say? 22:19
What more do you want me to say? You've obviously already made up your mind. I'm to blame, as usual. What's done is done. 22:21
But I want to talk about it because I feel bad. ☹ 22:23
Well, I think there is nothing to discuss. 22:23
I always do everything wrong. If you don't want to be with me, just tell me now and we'll break up sooner. 22:24
But I didn't say that. I do want to be with you. I love you very much. Please don't go thinking like that, it's not about that at all. 22:25
Write a message
Invalidation. Making comebacks to the questions that you receive, in an ironic tone can come across as very aggressive and invalidating to the other person.
Gaslighting. "Whatever you say, you live in your own little world."
Manipulative victim mentality.
Guilt. The person with the narcissistic personality has used this conversation to guilt-trip the other person into feeling blameworthy and selfish.

CONVERSELY, THE EMPATHIC PERSONALITY PROFILE IS FOUND AMONG PEOPLE WHO:

- Recognize, share, and understand others' emotions.
- Have a tendency to shoulder other people's responsibilities.
- Are helpful and want to provide emotional stability.
- Work hard and strive to improve themselves and the relationship as much as possible, and more (sacrifice).
- Show unconditional support.
- Tend to understand that we are all flawed human beings.
- Show willingness to be patient when it comes to another person's personal growth.
- Are under the misconception that everything will change in the relationship.
- Tend towards codependency. They have what I call a satellite complex.

SATELLITE COMPLEX

Your life revolves around another person and depends on what they are doing, thinking, or feeling.

Things that a person with an empathic personality profile might typically say include:

"I know my partner is not really like that."

"If they would just listen to me more, I'm sure everything would be different."

"I can get them to change, and then everything will go back to the way it was before."

Lara, for example, was a woman with an empathic personality profile who was in a relationship with Fernando, a man with a narcissistic personality profile.

Lara came into my office crying:

"María, I know he loves me, otherwise why would he have let me break up with my ex? We had talked about it and said we would both leave our respective relationships. The whole time he showed me that he really cared about me. We have been talking and meeting up practically every day since we first met. What I don't understand is why he is still with his partner after all this time. He does get angry and ignore me sometimes, because he says I bring him down, but then we go back to talking again, we'll meet up and everything is just like before. It's driving me crazy. He never used to be like this."

Lara was a woman in her 30s with a partner and no children, who had been in a secret relationship for three years with Fernando, a 34-year-old married man with two children. When they first met, they both had partners. They knew it wasn't right, but they got carried away with passion and ended up falling in love. After a year of carrying on like this, they sat down and talked. They decided that the best thing to do would be to leave their partners so they could be together. Following this conversation, Lara was true to her word, she immediately took the step of leaving her partner to be with Fernando. However, Fernando did not keep his promise. This was two years ago.

I'm not going to get into the moral nitty-gritty of whether what Lara and Fernando were doing with their respective partners was okay or not, because that's not the issue and my job is not to judge.

Throughout those two years, Lara waited patiently for Fernando to do as planned. She understood that it would take him longer than her, given his family situation.

Meanwhile, according to Lara, Fernando started reeling off a list of excuses:

"I'M UNHAPPY WITH MY WIFE, THAT'S WHY I WANT TO BE WITH YOU, BUT I DON'T KNOW HOW TO GO ABOUT IT YET."

Translation: I am unhappy with my wife and possibly want to leave her, but I don't dare. It's more comfortable to be with both of you, and preferable to maintain the status quo, so I can avoid facing a difficult situation. Also, it is easier to avoid Lara, who, if I decide I don't want to see her anymore, would be easier to leave than my wife, as we still live under the same roof.

Reality check: It is one thing to be unsure how to do something but another to refuse to do it. If the problem Fernando is alluding to is a true reflection of the situation, he could turn to a professional who could help guide him through it. What is not fair to Lara (or even to Fernando's wife) is to prolong the agony.

"I'M OVERWHELMED AND, AS SOON AS YOU ASK ME, I FEEL PRESSURED, WHICH MAKES ME FEEL EVEN MORE OVERWHELMED. I NEED TO TAKE MY TIME. PLEASE STOP ASKING ME."

Translation: It's your fault I'm not taking this step because you keep going on at me. If you didn't ask me to do it so much, I wouldn't feel so overwhelmed, and I would make my move sooner. You are the one who doesn't want us to be together.

Reality check: Lara has every right to ask about something they had both previously agreed upon. Fernando is flipping the script to give himself an excuse to be angry with Lara, making Lara feel that she was possibly being unreasonable.

But let's remember that Lara had been on the receiving end of these excuses for two years. Not weeks, nor months, but two whole years. This is important because, although those of us who work with couples do recognize that the emotional situations Fernando describes can indeed occur, two years of waiting, combined with his way of confronting the problem and communicating things, is abusive on his part.

"MY CHILDREN MISS YOU."

Translation: I don't want you to leave me, so I'm going to use my children to pull on your heartstrings. That way I'll still have an excuse to keep in touch, and you won't leave me.

"I CAN'T SEPARATE FROM MY WIFE BECAUSE OF WHAT IT WOULD DO TO MY CHILDREN."

Translation: Do you remember when I used my children to blur those boundaries you initially tried to set for me? Well, now I'm using the same excuse to get you to understand why I'm not leaving my wife. Are you going to put your needs in the relationship ahead of some children? How selfish are you?

Reality check: He's telling you exactly where you fit into his life. Lara knew Fernando's children as a "friend". In any case, children, whether shared or not, should never be used to resolve problems in a relationship between two adults.

"LET'S TAKE A BREAK FROM TALKING FOR A WHILE, SHALL WE? I WANT TO TEST THE WATERS BEFORE I FINALLY TAKE THAT STEP."

Translation: I feel the need to move on from you for a bit, but since I'm such a hot mess, I don't dare to actually leave you in case that just creates more problems, so I'm feeding you this utter nonsense line.

"LOOK, THAT'S IT, I'VE DECIDED. I LOVE YOU. YOU ARE THE LOVE OF MY LIFE AND I NEED TO TAKE THIS STEP. I'VE BEEN A SHIT THIS WHOLE TIME. I'M SORRY I'VE HURT YOU SO MUCH. I REALLY AM SORRY. I LOVE YOU."

Translation: What I think and feel is real, and right now I selfishly want all this for myself, basically ignoring everything you might be going through.

Reality check: I believe that Fernando at this moment, and I stress, only at this very moment, is being truthful. And I think this is the case because when he says it, there is always the possibility that he does actually feel that way. People with a narcissistic personality profile do not lack emotions. I never question how people feel (and I don't think anyone should judge whether someone else's feelings are true or not), so yes, I do think that Fernando probably loves Lara, but the reality of the situation, and considering how things are going to look further down the track, leads me to think that in general terms he loves her in his own particular way. A highly dysfunctional way at that, because there is such misalignment between what he says, feels, and does. This takes a toll on Lara because it fuels her uncertainty about the relationship. Fernando fails to comprehend the damage his attitude may be doing to Lara. He is incapable of showing even a minimum level of empathy towards her. Fernando has a narcissistic personality profile and narcissistic profiles, using their own logic, process things differently than empathic profiles. When viewed from the outside, there are things that empathic profiles just cannot compute because they try to approach things from an empathetic point of view. However, for someone with a narcissistic profile, all these responses have their own internal logic. That said, if we tried to process the way a narcissistic person thinks from an empathetic point of view, we wouldn't be able to see the logic in it anywhere. Doing so would be like trying to match the shape of a triangle to a circle. This is the logic that Lara just can't see, hence her feeling of "going crazy".

Empathic and narcissistic profiles do not appear only when interacting with each other, they are already ingrained from the home environment (remember the importance of personal history). At the end of this book we will bring all these concepts together when I talk about attachment theory.

"I know Fernando loves me," she said between sobs. "I just need him to listen to me and understand me."

"Lara, that would be ideal," I replied in one of our sessions. "I think that when he's listening to you, he hears your words, but he doesn't understand what you're saying. It's different."

Finally, since Fernando remained stubborn, Lara was the one who had to make the next move. After several months of therapy, she realized that she had no choice but to set very clear boundaries for Fernando and stay strong. Very, very strong.

We would take an idea and work solidly on it, which she'd then use to reflect on her own situation:

"Fernando, I love you and I have given everything for this relationship and for you, but I have realized that we can't go on like this and that it is getting us nowhere. Everything is very confusing and I do nothing but suffer. Because of this and seeing as you have no intention of changing your mind, even with all the opportunities we've been given, I have decided that I am ending this relationship for good."

As you can see, Fernando is not given an inch of wiggle room here. If, instead of giving this clear and resounding message, we had given this more empathetic one:

"Fernando, I love you and I have given everything for this relationship and for you, but I have realized that we can't go on like this and that it is getting us nowhere. Everything is very confusing, and I do nothing but suffer. Therefore, I would like to know if you are going to change your mind because, if not, I would like to end this relationship for good."

We would inadvertently have given Fernando an opening to say that he wants to be with Lara, and that he wants to try again one last time (although he's used this excuse a thousand times before).

BOUNDARIES

I'm going to illustrate the concepts of rejection and boundaries by using pears.

Imagine that someone offers you some of the best pears in the world to eat. However, you don't like pears, you prefer apples. So, you decide to reject the pears. There's nothing wrong with pears, you are only rejecting them because you prefer apples. The pears are still great. Someone else will surely come along who wants them, but in this case, you personally prefer apples.

Moral of the story # 1: If someone ever rejects you, the problem is not you.

Moral of the story # 2: You have the right to reject and set boundaries with someone, without fear of offending them.

So, whether you are rejected or boundaries are set for you, or whether you put boundaries in place for yourself, I want you to understand that these concepts have nothing at all to do with your personal worth as an individual. This is really important to wrap our heads around because, on the one hand, when we do it to others, we might feel guilty, and when we are the ones on the receiving end, we might feel that we are somehow unworthy of good things. But as you know, nothing could be further from the truth. So, if you have decided to set boundaries for someone or something (a boundary after all is a "no"), you must be aware that you are quite within your rights to do so and that, carrying on the metaphor, you are just a person who is starting to prefer apples.

If, after reading the previous chapter, you identify with the empathic profile, please know that the only way to maintain a healthy balance with someone who has a narcissistic profile is by setting very clear and assertive boundaries right from the outset. Lara had no choice but to set a definitive limit, since Fernando did not respect Lara's boundaries and Lara also let them get a little wobbly in the name of love, (remember the romantic myth "love conquers all"). Lara thought that love would change Fernando.

If you are not yet at this point, my advice is to put some boundaries in place straight away on the things which matter to you.

HERE ARE SOME EXAMPLES OF ASSERTIVELY COMMUNICATED BOUNDARIES:

- "I'm not going to give you my passwords nor will I let you go through my phone. Privacy is important, and I would like it to be respected in this relationship."
- "I would love to go to that restaurant we talked about today, but I'm feeling a bit low and would rather stay at home. We can plan it for next week."

- "I think this conversation is getting out of hand because we are starting to raise our voices. I'm going out for a few minutes to get some air. If it's all right with you, we can resume the conversation later when we're less heated."
- "Meeting up with my family and friends is important to me and I believe that maintaining some space to do things as individuals is necessary in every relationship."
- "I really appreciate your opinion, but I've been giving it some thought, and I think that the best thing for me is *X*."
- "I like you a lot, but I don't feel comfortable sexting or sending nudes."
- "To me that is no joke. I find it offensive. Please don't say that again."
- "I'd love it if, when we're together, we're not looking at our phones or TV screens so we can just enjoy the moment."
- "For me, using condoms is non-negotiable. I want to do it with a condom, and if not, I'd rather not do anything."

If, after reading the description of these profiles, you think you match the narcissistic personality profile, please know that I don't blame you. This is not about who's a good guy and who's a bad guy. It's important to make that clear because many people consider that having a narcissistic personality profile equates to being a bad person, and that having an empathic profile indicates a good person.

My job as a psychologist is not to say who is good or bad, or what is right or wrong. It is to differentiate between what is functional and what is dysfunctional. Every behavior, thought, emotion, or attitude is a response to a person's background, among other things. Nobody chooses one hundred percent of what happens to them in life, especially during childhood.

No one is born choosing their parents, places in the world to be born, or which cultures to grow up in. No one. That is why I believe that there is an explanation for everything, because everything has an origin and a backstory, however I also believe that not everything can be justified.

You most certainly have had a past, which to some extent informs and explains your attitude. But that doesn't absolve you from having to change certain aspects of your behavior within relationships, or from learning that you are not the "boss" when in a couple. You may also have to discard many beliefs about love and learn to respect certain boundaries.

So far, I have spoken about the narcissistic profile as if it were one-dimensional, but I have done so in general terms because, to be precise, there are actually many types, and depending on the type and its defining characteristics, their capacity for awareness of the things they do can vary (some are depraved in the things they do and say). Some narcissistic profiles also display serious psychopathy (a trait that, according to research, is less related to the environment and personal background, and seems to be more of a biological issue). There are also people with narcissistic profiles who may have a narcissistic personality disorder (this is a clinical diagnosis that, although it shares similar traits to those described, its set of symptoms is much more complex and even severe in some cases), but also, within this variability, there are those whose attitudes are somewhat more moderate.

It's all much more complex than it seems.

In my experience, these more moderate profiles usually have a better prognosis in therapy and display some interest in learning other ways of behaving, as well as maintaining their interest in changing over time (this is what we know as the classic narcissistic profile). They may never fully understand their partner, but once they understand the logic behind relationships, they learn to make very different comments to those that Fernando made to Lara, and they understand that, sometimes, it is important to stop navel-gazing and look further ahead.

Please don't take this as some kind of message of hope towards all cases and situations. Often it is hope for change which keeps the person with an empathic profile stuck in the relationship. I don't know what your particular circumstances are, but please know that, although people can change, it doesn't happen simply by wanting to. It's one thing to want to change, it's another to be able to. And believe me, love, although it is a necessary condition, is not the only condition for wanting or being able to change.

If, after reading this section, you feel that you have more of an empathic personality profile, I want you to know that sometimes the only thing left to do is to set the ultimate boundary in a relationship by breaking up.

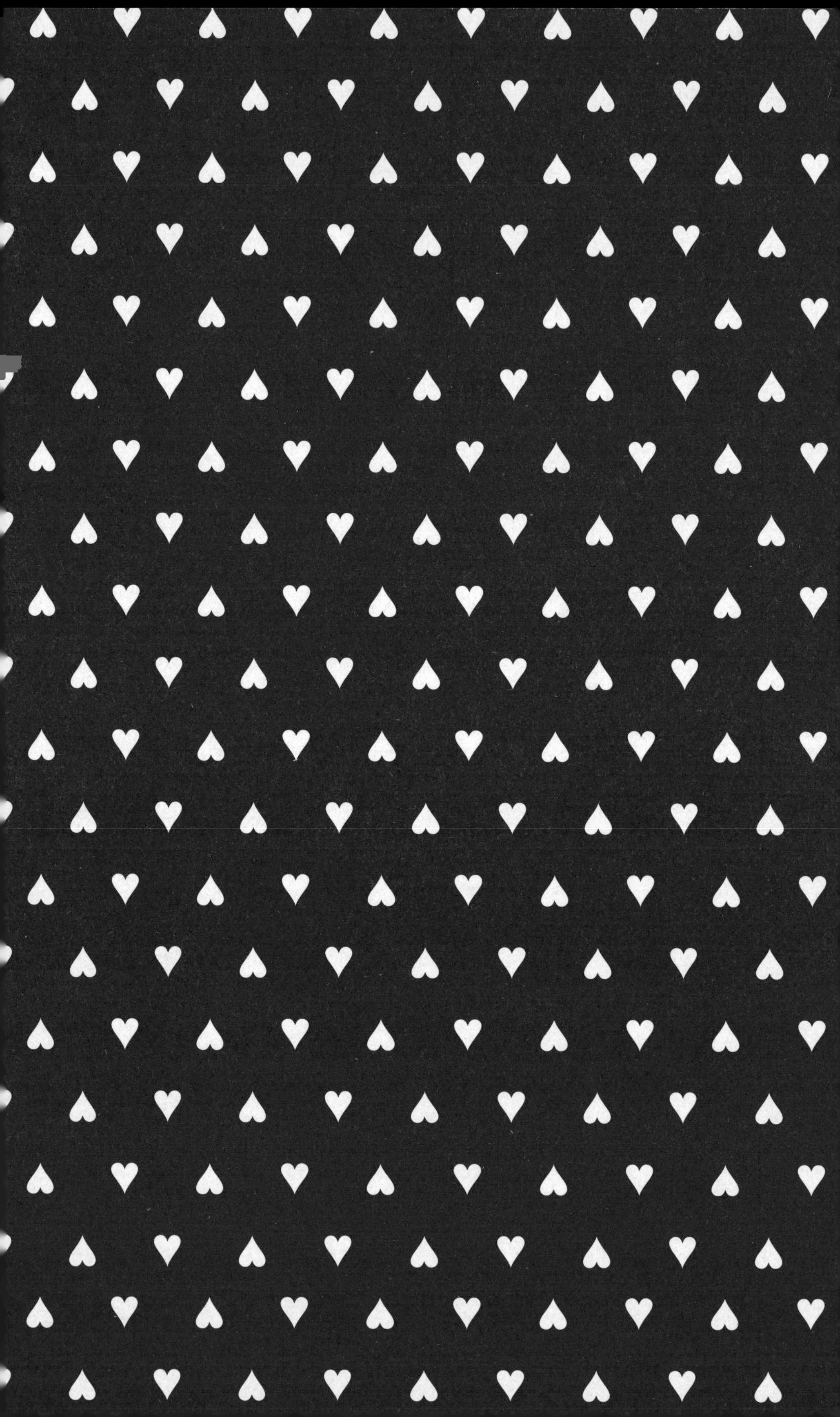

♥ 9 ♥

DEPENDENT BREAKUPS

Dependent breakups are not normal breakups. Nor is the fallout from them. Everything is much more difficult. Everything. Considering that the best decision for everyone is to end the relationship comes at an unimaginable cost. I won't lie to you, this is a painful process. But what's more painful than being with someone who doesn't actually make you happy? Eventually, you'll come to understand that what you have now, which is only sometimes good, is not love. You haven't yet experienced true love; and believe me, you will find it. You will enjoy it, and you will finally know what it feels like to be deeply loved, firsthand, because something inside of you, deep down, will intuit that this love feels like home. One you will undoubtedly never wish to leave.

Once you make the decision to make a clean break, you must bear in mind that there is no turning back; you need to be very sure of what you are about to do. I'm not asking you to be one hundred percent sure and to be guided only by reason, because I know that's impossible, but at the very least you need to be very clear in your own mind about the reasons for the breakup. My advice is to write down the pros and cons of both staying in the relationship and breaking it off. This will help cut through any brain fog so that you can get a clearer picture of the situation.

PROS OF STAYING IN THE RELATIONSHIP	CONS OF STAYING IN THE RELATIONSHIP
PROS OF LEAVING THE RELATIONSHIP	**CONS OF LEAVING THE RELATIONSHIP**

I can't guarantee that you'll be crystal clear about what you want to do with your relationship after this exercise, but seeing things in writing always helps, and besides, it's using a higher level of cognitive processing.

I always say that there are three levels of expression, ranging from the most basic to the most complex.

LEVELS OF EXPRESSION:

- **Level 1:** Thinking. This is the most basic level of processing. At this level, when trying to process complex things, we find they seem to go round and round in our minds, incessantly. They will most likely keep going round aimlessly, as if lost in space.

- **Level 2:** Speaking. At this level, the brain requires more energy to process things. Our speech requires order and coherence in order to be understood by others. Have you ever been thinking about something, but then the moment it comes out of your mouth it suddenly makes no sense? Some things do seem to sound better, more catastrophic, or immediate in our heads.
- Level 3: Writing. This takes place at a higher level of consciousness. In order to write we must expend more energy and cognitive resources. What we're trying to communicate must be articulated clearer than in thought or speech. When applied to emotions and thoughts, this makes them more easily understood, not only because of the effort it takes to capture and express it in words, but also because once we have reflected on everything, we may be struck by a sudden flash of insight.

Do you remember when we were kids and we were given math problems that we would have to read and reread four, five, or six times and we still didn't understand them? As I write this I feel as if I am still in that primary school classroom, trying to figure out what on earth that textbook was asking me to do. What do you mean the middle sister is three years younger than Mark and Mark is twice the age of little Josh, who is seven years old? I remember that when I asked my teacher for help, she'd say, "Let's see, read it out loud," and I, all motivated, read the problem in front of the whole class. Sometimes, after reading it aloud I'd say "Aaah, now I get it, now I know." Why? What had happened there? Most likely, until then, my brain had been turning over this same idea without success, but as soon as I made that content "real" through speech, my brain had to expend more resources on this action. Of course, even then, I still didn't understand what the problem was asking me to do! My teacher would take me up to the blackboard to go over it step-by-step, even doing little drawings to help explain what the problem was about. Once again, more brain resources required equals increased brain activity, leading to a better understanding of the subject. As soon as I had the whole problem drawn out, with diagrams, I understood what needed to be done and found the answer quickly.

♥

INTUITIVE DECISIONS

The same thing happens with our emotions. The more we think about them, the fewer solutions we find; and in fact, the opposite can happen too: we can find ourselves in a state of mental block called analysis paralysis.

Analysis paralysis is a phenomenon that happens to us more often than we'd like. When we go over the same thing again and again, non-stop, there comes a point where our brain becomes obsessed with those ideas and we literally crash. When experiencing this type of mental block, anxiety symptoms may even appear, such as a feeling of suffocation, chest pain, headaches, and nausea, among others. It is as if, in amongst all those ideas, memories, and predictions, the brain gets lost and starts meandering around, with no way out. When this happens to the brain, it is unable to activate any proper defense mechanisms. For the brain, not finding solutions indicates that there are no other possible options. That's when mental block sets in.

How, then, can we come to the right conclusions without falling into analysis paralysis? The other option would be to act upon emotions, but acting on emotions is almost always a mistake, as our feelings are changeable, they come and go, and are often the cause of impulsive behavior. As Eduard Punset said in his book *La intuición no es irracional* (*Intuition is not irrational*), we have to act upon intuition, which is a mixture of reason and emotion.

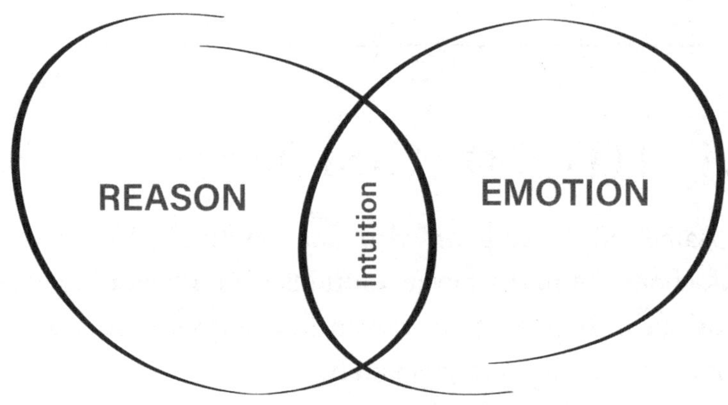

Intuition is a type of knowledge which is not solely formed from following the rational path. It is the ability to know, understand, or perceive something clearly and immediately.

In healthcare we talk a lot about the “clinical eye”. The clinical eye can be a good example of intuition.

Another good example of making a decision by intuition is the decision to get married. (I know this is the opposite of what we are trying to work on, but I think this helps to clearly illustrate what I mean when I talk about intuition.)

If getting married was something decided solely based on logic and reason, we would have dozens of reasons never to get married, given that there are so many things that could go wrong. If, on the other hand, it were something decided solely on emotions, we would all be getting married barely three days after meeting our partner. Most people get married based on intuition. There is something whispering in their ear that tells them it will all work out. And they charge right ahead! (Then some people discover that they don't know how to handle a relationship, but that's another matter entirely.)

And how is intuitive decision making done? To reach the most accurate conclusion, you don't need to go over and over and over it in your head forever. Just think about it a couple of times, talk about it a couple more times, and write it down a few times (or even draw it, which requires an even higher level of cognition). Once we've thoroughly gone over it in our heads, we sleep on it for a few days, distract our minds, and do things that make us feel good: we meet up with friends, pursue our hobbies, take long showers, go for walks, run, masturbate, laugh, cry, and even work. And then, suddenly, one day, it all becomes clear. That's how our minds work.

This is what people mean when they say they "just knew". It is neither a thought, nor an emotion, it's a feeling. Those of you who have worked on your intuition and are very in tune with it will know what I mean. If, after this decision-making process, you start ruminating over the same issue again, it is likely that you have ignored your intuition, and reason has taken over again, with all the consequences that entails. So, my advice is that once you've made an intuitive decision, make a list of all the reasons that led you towards that decision instead of another.

EXERCISE:

Make a list of all the reasons why you decided to end the relationship.

The idea is that you keep it in mind all the time. I recommend that you always carry it with you. If you write it on paper, fold it up and carry it in your bag, between the pages of your diary, or in your wallet. If you write it down electronically, carry it around with you on your mobile phone. Later on, I will explain why this is extremely necessary.

Warning: do not confuse intuition with anxiety or fear. We commonly do this because we can interpret the physical signs of anxiety or fear as signs of intuition, however nothing could be further from the truth. Some people describe intuition as "a feeling in the stomach or chest" but remember that one of the symptoms of anxiety is precisely a feeling of emptiness, a sense of pressure on the chest, difficulty breathing, digestive problems, or a knot in the stomach.

I'll explain why this happens. When you are thinking about making a decision that may affect your future, you try to decide based on what you think will happen. This is your brain activating a mechanism called "anticipation", which consists of trying to visualize what may lie ahead. This mechanism is triggered by fear of the unknown (the future). The brain, as if it has a life of its own, says "Hey, how come I don't know what will happen in the future? And how am I supposed to know how to prepare for whatever might happen? How will I be able to control my environment? Ah, I know! I'll anticipate it, but I'll do it in a negative and catastrophic way, just in case. You always have to be prepared for the worst." And that's how your brain tries to spare you from exposure to possible pain or suffering. This gives rise to anxiety, which is nothing more than a physical and mental response to the brain's catastrophic and negative anticipations. This way of processing things, although the result of rational processing, can be distorted by certain irrational beliefs. For example, I may strongly believe that my partner is being unfaithful without having any empirical evidence to prove it, other than my own suspicions, and the way I interpret what my partner says and does (remember the triangle and the tricks the brain plays with interpretations).

"And what if I'm right about what's going to happen?" you may be wondering. Making the correct guess among many potential outcomes is not the result of intuition, but rather it springs from the mixture of anxiety and fear which was responsible for that anticipated outcome. Nor is being right about what will happen in the future a sign of having a "sixth sense", as the result may be purely down to probability. For example, if you think of 37 possibilities, it is not unusual to get one right, since the more possibilities you anticipate, the more likely you are to land on the correct one.

When you want to distinguish between anxiety and intuition, remember that intuition . . .

. . . is neither purely the result of reason nor of irrational beliefs.

. . . does not come from your past knowledge or experiences.

. . . does not tell you which path not to take, but which path to take (it does not prevent, it motivates).

. . . is not accompanied by fear.

. . . does not come from a need to know the future.

BREAKING UP

When the bond in a relationship is dependent, there cannot be a full stop and a new paragraph. It must always end definitively. Always. A couple who has maintained a dependent relationship will continue to maintain a dependent relationship, no matter how much time passes or whatever form it takes.

Can I stay friends with my ex? What about a friends with benefits arrangement?

Absolutely not. Neither option is viable.

When we break up with someone, we might consider these possibilities because we believe it is preferable to have at least a friendship or a sexual encounter from time to time than to have nothing at all. And, okay, this might be viable if you two had a healthy relationship. But you don't have a healthy relationship because, if you did, you wouldn't be reading this book.

Friendship following a toxic relationship does not exist. Friendships provide emotional support, requiring trust and mutual care. Think about it: you didn't receive any of that, at least not in any stable way, during the relationship, so why would it suddenly come along after the breakup? Also, even if that were the case, someone you only meet up with for sex is not a friend. Which brings us to the next point.

Some people justify meeting up with their ex for sex because it's the only good thing they had together during the relationship. To which I would say that if it's already difficult to separate sex from emotions, imagine if these encounters were with an ex with whom you have a toxic bond.

That dependent bond will always exist between the two of you. No matter how much time goes by. Once two people have learned to relate to each other in a particular way, those learned patterns are forever ingrained, no matter what form the relationship takes.

If you try because you somehow still believe that this won't happen to you, or that your relationship is different or special, I predict that you are very likely to fall into the trap of the dependent breakup cycle which we'll talk about in more detail later.

I know this all sounds a bit radical, but I assure you it's not. I've seen couples who have tried to be "friends" after a breakup, and all they've done is end up worse off than they were before, and prolonging the suffering. People in dependent relationships can never be friends after they break up.

I know that right now you might still be a bit skeptical. I know this because, as you know, I was in your shoes too a few years ago. Every time a man made me feel humiliated, I became angry and thought about how I didn't deserve such treatment. However, despite being at rock bottom, I was unable to detach myself from those relationships, and, one by one, they consumed me emotionally until I had internalized the belief that I was someone unworthy of love. And so, by degrees, I slowly lost myself and sold out emotionally in exchange for a little attention from the opposite sex. I don't think anything has ever made me feel so stupid. Perhaps it's this behavior of mine that I still blame myself the most for today. Are you familiar with that feeling of being to blame when you mentally replay all those situations in your head that, today, with the benefit of hindsight, seem completely different from how they seemed in the moment?

Well, that's what happens to me. And I confess that it's one of the hardest things I still have to cope with: the guilt and anger that come from feeling like I could have "loved" myself a bit more, and handled things differently. Now I am lucky enough to understand that my inability to cut things off at the root was not a voluntary choice. It's not that I didn't "deserve" love. I am one hundred percent certain that it wasn't about that.

"We can be friends," he said. Friends for what? Now I know: to have an excuse to latch onto when craving the relationship.

This inability to end relationships, believe me, doesn't come out of nowhere. The intermittent reinforcement you get from them has a lot to answer for. When things are going well, they're going very well. You know what I'm talking about. For me, everything was magical, like something out of a fairy tale (maybe that was the problem). Such perfection and outpourings of love from the other person made me feel like I was their priority, which, when these things are generally a bit scarce in the relationship, you receive and appreciate with open arms, as if it's going to be the last time.

This is what happened to Adele, a patient who was in therapy with me for two years. We spent one of those years working on trying to find the middle ground between emotion and reason, which, as you know, is what we call listening to our intuition.

She left the sessions feeling motivated and determined to leave her partner. However, after a few days she would return, having doubts. The sessions were spent talking about the things her partner did to her and how hurt she felt when the person she had loved most made her feel worthless. Adele said that one of the things that made her doubt things the most was that, as much as her partner treated her badly, he would later try to shower her with gifts and attention. These mixed messages kept Adele staying with her partner and unsure what she should do about the relationship. When the moment of truth came, her mind would turn to mush and she'd bottle out. In our sessions, she told me that just when she was able to see things clearly, those positive memories would come flooding back and make her decide to keep quiet and continue fighting for the relationship.

"I'm staying for the sake of my children"

Oh, the number of times I have heard this in my clinic! Countless times! I know it's really hard to imagine a separation when you're experiencing it from the perspective of your own pain. But that's your pain, not your children's. And you're using it to make this decision.

That's illogical when we consider that the relationship you have with your partner is just that; it's your relationship, not your children's. Your children will always be your children, and you will always be their parents, whether you are together or separated.

It is true that the main concern expressed by parents in counseling is that their children will suffer due to the changes, or that they'll live in a hostile environment. But none of this has to happen if a separation is handled correctly. Children tend to adapt to new situations quickly. So, if you have children, please know that they don't need their parents to be together, they just need their parents to be happy. Plus, if a child sees their adult caregiver and emotional refuge for when times get tough, remaining calm and emotionally stable, then they learn to trust that everything will be okay. If, on the other hand, the child sees these adults lacking emotional stability, constantly in turmoil, fighting all the time, and that the atmosphere at home is hostile, the child will feel that everything is wrong, like anything can happen at any moment (uncertainty, "waiting for the other shoe to drop"); they will feel unprotected, that they cannot trust anyone, and that their parents are unpredictable, which equates to emotional distress. Such distress can carry on into adolescence and adulthood (although some children display symptoms earlier).

You have no idea how many patients with a history of non-separated parents confess to me that seeing their parents so unhappy together, during childhood or adolescence, resulted in a more distant relationship with them, and pushed them to seek refuge in other people, outside of the family environment. And that's the best-case scenario.

Sticking it out for the kids and believing it is the best decision may well be an example of emotional reasoning. Emotional reasoning is a form of cognitive distortion (that is, a mental pattern which is clouded by perceptions, which are in turn colored by the person's own experiences and learning). Emotional reasoning in this case would be reaching a conclusion conditioned by how you feel. "Isn't that normal?" you might ask. Well, no, that is why it is considered a distortion. In other words, when we use emotional reasoning, we lack information or a solid argument to support it.

I'll give you another example.

Imagine that you have just broken up with your partner, with whom you have been quite disappointed, and you now think that "all men/all women are the same." That statement is incoherent, isn't it? You don't know everyone on this planet, so you can't say they are all the same. This conclusion is drawn from a place of pain; therefore, we'd consider this to be emotional reasoning. The same goes for the title of this section. "I'm staying for the sake of my children" is an example of emotional reasoning because it stems from your pain, and because once analyzed, we see that this belief easily falls apart.

NO CONTACT

Going "no contact" is the most important technique for overcoming emotional dependence, and it is either applied completely or not at all. The reason is simple: if not applied properly, it doesn't work.

The idea behind "no contact" is the premise that by removing any stimuli associated with your partner from your life, you avoid prolonging any psychological suffering from the breakup and also swerve the intermittent on-again-off-again patterns of breaking up and getting back together again (I will expand upon this later).

How do I go no contact?

I'm going to explain step by step how to go no contact. But first, I want you to say goodbye to your ex for good, with self-respect and respect for what you've been through. This is vital, and I know this first-hand, both from my own experience and from what my patients tell me during their sessions.

Remember that what we do in haste, we almost always repent at leisure; so, it's essential to do the exercise I'm about to suggest, being aware of each step.

Your brain (and, why not say it, your heart as well) needs to feel that it is "letting go" and moving on from something; in other words, it needs space and time to grieve. Grief is a word associated with the emotional adjustment process that we go through following a loss, and although the person you have left is not dead, psychologically speaking, it is as if they were. Therefore, it is necessary to respect the grieving process, with all its ups and downs, for as long as it takes.

MEMORY BOX

To bring something into our consciousness, we need to perform a ritual. Yes, you read that right. When a loved one dies, a wake and a funeral are held with a service, that is, a ritual that, depending on the religion or culture, will be performed in one way or another. For your farewell, you won't need to hold a wake or a service, but you will need to hold a burial. Let's go through it step by step.

STEP 1

Gather together all the mementos you have of this person and your relationship with them. Photos, bus tickets, cinema tickets, soft toys, T-shirts, figurines, etc.

Anything is welcome for this exercise. You can export your WhatsApp conversations from the app itself and email them to yourself in text format. It's easy: open the conversation with that person, tap on the three dots in the top right corner, and then tap "More" in the options that appear, then tap "Export chat". You will be given the option to export multimedia files too, i.e. photos, videos, audio files, etc., in case you want to save everything. Once you have selected the option you want, you can choose which platform you want to send the conversation to. I recommend Gmail. Once you have completed this process, you will receive an email with all your conversations (and photos/videos, if you have included them). If you want, you can download this file and save it to a hard drive, so you can delete the email and not have to see it every time you access your inbox.

STEP 2

Put all those memories in a cardboard/wooden/metal box.

STEP 3

Once you have put everything in the box, you have to "bury" it. Just hiding it somewhere difficult to access will work (for example, a cupboard you hardly ever open) or at least make sure you don't leave it out in plain sight.

The idea is to keep everything stored away for now. This exercise doesn't involve throwing away your memories because, if you do, you will feel like you are getting rid of a part of your past, and your past is yours, it's a part of your life. Besides, throwing away your memories right now would probably be too painful.

This exercise serves to tell your brain, "You have to say goodbye to this, but look, I'm leaving it here; I'm not going to throw it away, so you can see it whenever you want." This way, your brain is more "at peace" because, although you probably won't open that box ever again and might even throw it away once you've got over the relationship, if you present the idea of "never seeing these things again" to your mind right from the start, it will only cause greater anxiety. Although if you have an attic like the one in *Charmed*, you might not mind keeping the box forever. It's up to you.

Now then, we're ready to continue.

Tips on how to go no contact "well"

TIP 1: BLOCK AND DELETE YOUR EX FROM YOUR SOCIAL MEDIA.

Yes, you have to both block and delete them. It's not enough to just delete or to mute them. And when I say social media, I mean all of them: Facebook, Twitter, Instagram, WhatsApp, YouTube, Telegram . . . everything.

This needs to be so radical because you cannot leave even a single opportunity available to re-establish contact with this person. If the door is left even slightly ajar, then the attempt to go no contact will all be for nothing. All it takes is one of those moments of weakness (e.g. being at home on a Sunday after watching a romantic film and letting your mind wander back to that person) to break your abstinence streak.

Remember that this is like trying to break an addiction.

TIP 2: DO NOT CALL OR SEND TEXT MESSAGES.

Block their number. If necessary, delete their number from your phone, or change yours, to prevent that person from contacting you, or you from contacting them again.

My advice is to delete all your conversations and photos with them which are stored on your phone, and once you've done that, delete their number from your contacts. Remember: before taking this step, do the Memory Box exercise.

TIP 3: DO NOT MEET UP WITH THEIR FRIENDS AND/OR FAMILY.

Even if you have a good relationship with them, once you have said goodbye to those closest to you, it is best not to meet up with them or talk to them again, at least for the time being. At this point, meeting up with them would be tantamount to indirectly reminding yourself of your ex.

TIP 4: DON'T IMPULSIVELY GO TO SEE THEM.

Think twice and then wait until the next day. In the meantime, your emotions will settle down, logic will take over, and you will realize that you don't actually want to. Give that a try.

TIP 5: DON'T TALK ABOUT YOUR EX AND ASK OTHERS NOT TO TALK ABOUT THEM EITHER.

I'm referring to comments such as "I saw your ex at so-and-so's with so-and-so", or questions about the other person's life. Think about it: how exactly does receiving this kind of information help you move through your grieving process? Exactly.

TIP 6: FOR THE TIME BEING, AVOID PLACES WHERE YOU MIGHT BUMP INTO THEM.

You'll have time to go back to those places in future if you want to.

The brain associates memories with things like places, smells, tastes, and people, etc. Have you ever eaten a dessert that reminded you of your childhood? Have you ever caught a whiff of perfume that reminded you of a family member? What do you think will happen, then, with those places you used to frequent with your ex? Emotions are aroused in the brain in response to any stimulus that triggers a memory. So, the further away you can keep stimuli which reminds you of the other person, the better. Even if that means, for now, you have to change your plans or can't go about your normal daily life. In the long run, you will get back to your routines, I assure you, but right now, if you really want to take that step, then your brain needs to get away from all that stimuli and you need to grieve.

Some people, when they hear these tips, ask me if all this won't make the grieving process worse. They are afraid of never getting their life back, so they believe that the best thing to do is to keep living their life as usual, without breaking contact with anything or anyone (apart from their ex), as if nothing had happened. Their justification for this is firmly rooted in pride: "I'm not going to let this person affect my life anymore." But the reality is far from this. Unfortunately, holding onto this belief usually achieves the opposite. The more contact we have with the other person, directly or indirectly, the more their influence will seep into our lives.

There are other people who believe that the best thing to do is to constantly "test" themselves to see if they have any lingering feelings for the other person. This is also a bad idea. Life is not a game where you must constantly test yourself. Would you go running while recovering from a broken ankle? No? So why would you during the grieving process? As you can see, it's absurd, but I don't blame anyone for holding these beliefs; emotional education in our culture is sorely lacking.

Sometimes, there are situations where going no contact is difficult due to the circumstances (for example, a couple with children and shared custody, or a relationship between colleagues, etc.).

However, as far as possible, you should still try to put it into practice. For example, if you maintain a civil relationship with your ex-partner because you have children together, but you want to go no contact, then keep conversations with your ex-partner solely and exclusively limited to matters concerning your children. As soon as the conversation or situation turns to more emotional or sentimental topics that you think might hurt you, end the interaction. As you can see, in this scenario going no contact only applies to the most emotional aspects.

I have sometimes been asked if refusing to engage in these situations or conversations constitutes ghosting, and the answer is no.

Remember that for it to be ghosting, there must be a certain degree of affective responsibility between you. In a relationship where responsibility is limited purely to caring for children, given that this is the only bond that keeps the two parties together, and therefore communication is necessary for this to be carried out effectively, there is no emotional affective responsibility. Therefore, not responding or withdrawing from the conversation when you are not interested because it is turning into something more emotional does not constitute ghosting. You are fully within your rights to stop responding, to disappear, and to ignore the other person as you deem fit (so long as it's not to evade your responsibilities towards your own children). The same goes for colleagues. If your dependent relationship is with a colleague, you will have to maintain contact for work-related matters, but for anything not strictly work-related, you can most certainly turn a deaf ear.

The difficulties of maintaining no contact:

The grief that comes with dependent relationships is enormous. One day you're fine, you feel strong and like you can take on the world, and the next you're in a terrible slump, crying in the corner and feeling like nothing makes sense. Grief is hard enough and complicated by itself, but this . . . oh dear, this is on another level.

At first, you spend a few days (or weeks) feeling like a poor lost soul. You don't feel like leaving the house, you don't feel like doing anything, and you don't want to see anyone. All you know is that you want to get back together with that person.

Suddenly, one day everything seems fine, you feel strong, energetic and supported by friends and family who know what's going on. You're absolutely certain there's no way on earth you would ever go back to your ex. The next day (or it may even be just a few hours later), you're back to feeling low. You can't stop thinking about that person, how much you love them and all the good memories you share. The idea that they might already be seeing someone else, or that they have forgotten you, flits across your mind. This triggers your attachment system (basically the control tower that sends signals of possible "abandonment" and perceived "danger to survival" – in evolutionary terms – to the brain) and you think it's a good idea to get their attention back in some way (protest behavior). At times like these, pride sometimes takes over (thank goodness, in these cases), but at other times desire wins out. So, you do it, and you fall down that rabbit hole again.

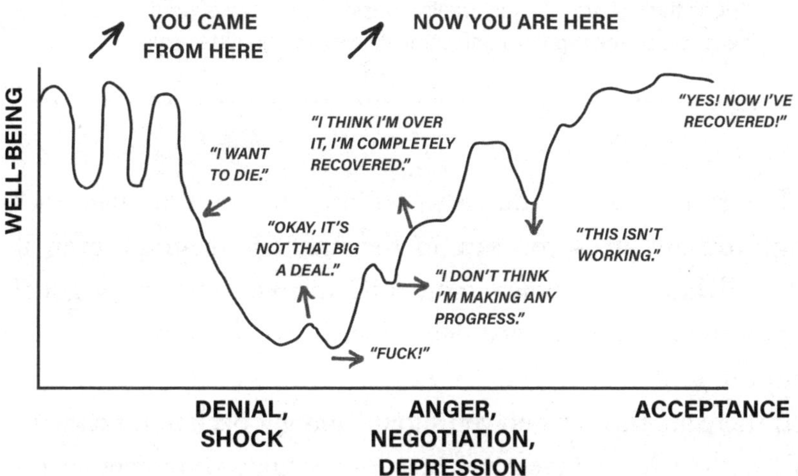

It is often said that there are five stages of grief, however we have the difficulty here that all the studies conducted on grief so far have been based on the actual loss of family members and loved ones. So, I'm going to tell you about what I see in my practice, which tends to unfold in a series of stages.

- **Shock. Denial:** This is the first stage immediately after the final break-up, when you are flooded with emotions. You are in such a bad place emotionally that you feel you've hit rock bottom. This is totally normal; your brain is still processing the loss and is unsure what is happening.
- **Anger. Negotiation. Depression:** All at once. During this stage you are extremely angry with your ex, but then find you suddenly miss them and must wrestle with yourself not to message them again. Then the anger returns as you recall how bad the relationship made you feel, your sadness, and awareness of your newfound situation. This is just an example, to illustrate that if the relationship itself was an emotional rollercoaster, it will be even more so now.
- **Acceptance:** Acceptance of the breakup. You no longer feel attached. You feel indifferent. You're glad you ended the relationship, even if it meant going through this really rocky period for a while. This is the last stage. I don't really consider it a stage of grief because, by the time this one comes along, the grief has passed.

The fact is, by assiduously working through it, whatever stage you are at as you saw in the previous diagram, even if you still have your down moments, you will still see gradual improvements. It is a very slow process, but I promise you, it's worth it.

If there are times when you slip up and get back in touch with your ex, how bad you feel and how long it takes you to get over it will depend on many factors. These include your own personality, characteristics of the relationship, the other person's reaction, and the way in which you're working on these issues yourself. This last factor carries a lot of weight, but it is not decisive if, for example, your ex is harassing or stalking you (fortunately, this is not the case in most situations, although it does happen). Don't think it's purely a matter of willpower alone.

Remember when I mentioned withdrawal symptoms? Most of my patients talk about the difficulty of maintaining no contact. Of course, if we consider that the relationship is essentially like a drug you're addicted to, who could resist taking a little bit? Mistakenly thinking "I'm in control", we believe that nothing will happen if we talk or meet up with that person. But this couldn't be further from the truth. Something does happen (and it happens a lot). Imagine that someone who is detoxing from cocaine in a rehabilitation center, in the midst of withdrawal, thinks it's okay to take a *little line* to calm the cravings, justifying it by saying that they are "in control". That doesn't seem logical, does it? In fact, what's more likely is that following that *little line*, the person will enter a downward spiral of drug use and end up right back where they started. Well, the same thing happens with dependent relationships, obvious differences aside. There is no chemical substance, true, but I would remind you that certain stimuli generate the same molecules in the brain as those which are released when taking a drug.

"Isn't that avoidance? What if I run into my ex again and feel even worse because I've been avoiding them all this time?" my patients sometimes ask. To which I always reply that it's not avoidance, and for example, they won't feel worse if they happen to bump into them on the street.

I'm not saying that if it happens, you won't be caught off guard, but once you've detoxed from the bond, you won't feel anything on a romantic level if you've gone no contact properly, and if enough time has passed. (This is easily identifiable: enough time has passed when you feel that your ex, in terms of being a partner, doesn't give a damn about you in the slightest.)

The way to work on emotional dependency is similar to working on an addiction to a substance or a videogame. No psychologist or psychiatrist worth their salt would ever let a patient continue using drugs, for example, while in rehab. That doesn't mean that patients will always necessarily start using again. Any relapse would be down to other factors, but certainly not because they gave up drugs during the detoxification process.

This too shall pass, trust me. I promise you that one day you'll get back to a place of emotional stability and calm, but you must stay strong, have compassion for yourself, and be patient with the situation. Whatever happens, press on. Giving these things time is essential, however time, by itself, does nothing; you still have to work on yourself.

No contact must be as strict as possible, and although sometimes you may not be able to avoid breaking it, you shall try your very best.

As you have already seen, slipping up is easily done, but to make the slope a bit less slippery, there is a tool I can give you which may help.

This tool is governed by a very important principle: there is no point in getting anywhere near things that could trigger us.

How are you going to do it? I'll help you. Take the following steps. Firstly, you need to make two lists.

The first will be a list of situations you want to avoid.

THINGS I WANT TO AVOID:

EXAMPLES: TALKING TO MY EX, MEETING UP WITH MY EX, SLEEPING WITH MY EX, GETTING BACK TOGETHER WITH MY EX, ETC.

NOW IT'S YOUR TURN:

The second will be a list of all the things you can think of which cause you to tumble back into the situations described in the list of things you want to avoid.

THINGS THAT LURE ME INTO THE SITUATIONS I WANT TO AVOID:

EXAMPLES: GOING OUT PARTYING, DRINKING ALCOHOL, AND HAVING MY MOBILE PHONE HANDY, WATCHING ROMANTIC FILMS, WALKING DOWN *X* STREET, GOING INTO *X* SHOP, GOING INTO *X* BAR, LISTENING TO *X* SONG, SEEING THEIR NAME ON A POSTER, HEARING STORIES ABOUT LONG-DISTANCE COUPLES GETTING BACK TOGETHER, A MEMORY OF WHEN WE WERE TOGETHER POPPING INTO MY MIND, ETC.

NOW IT'S YOUR TURN:

All this information is invaluable to you. It will all help you get to your "point of no return".

THE POINT OF NO RETURN:

THE POINT OF NO RETURN IS A THEORY USED IN PSYCHOLOGY WHEN WORKING ON IMPULSE CONTROL.

IT CAN BE REPRESENTED AS FOLLOWS:

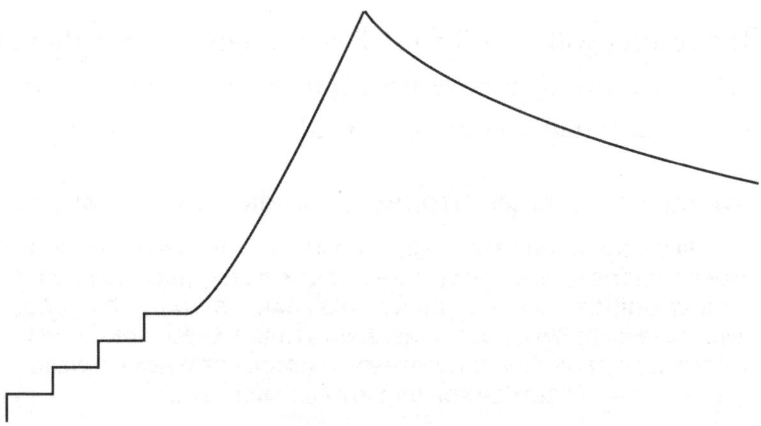

In this little drawing, each step represents an emotionally charged stimulus. Thus, each step corresponds to each of the things you have described in your list of things that lure you into the situations you want to avoid.

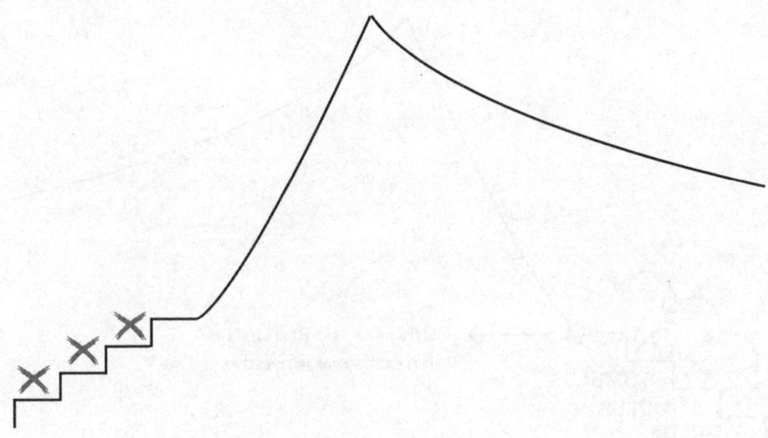

As you can see in the diagram, these stimuli all add up (like climbing steps), adding emotional intensity to the moment before you "slip up", that is, the moment before your behavior gets out of control.

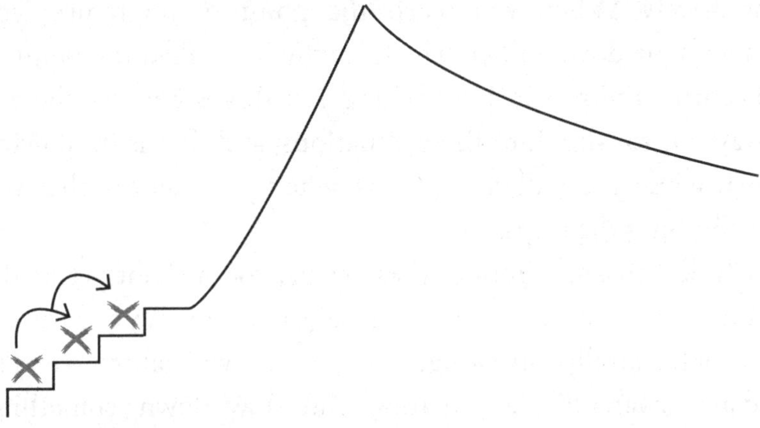

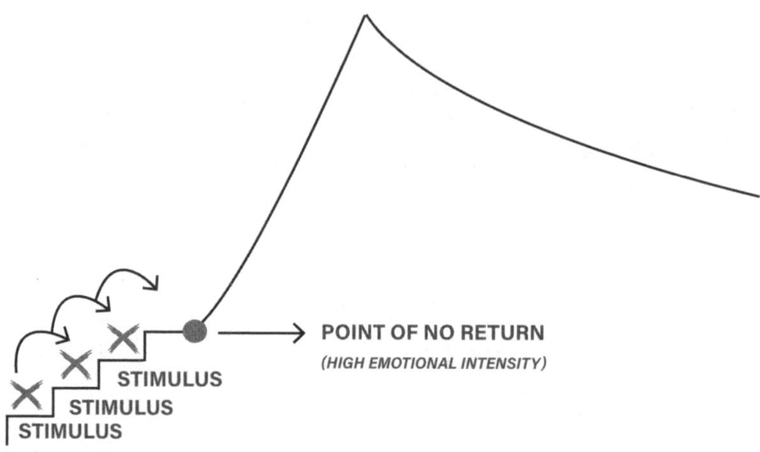

The point of no return in this case is a point at which, once you have accumulated a great deal of emotional intensity, there is no turning back. The only option is for the intensity to rapidly increase until you act completely emotionally and impulsively. When you reach the point of no return, you cannot slow down either, which is why it is called the point of no return. The reason I am telling you this is because there is a way not to "slip" into these situations, and that is by slowing down while you still can. That is, when you identify that you are climbing the steps.

While you are climbing these steps, you are not yet at the point of no return, so physiologically, emotionally, cognitively, and behaviorally speaking, your body will allow you to become aware of the situation and slow down, something that is otherwise impossible, and here's why; your amygdala is being hijacked.

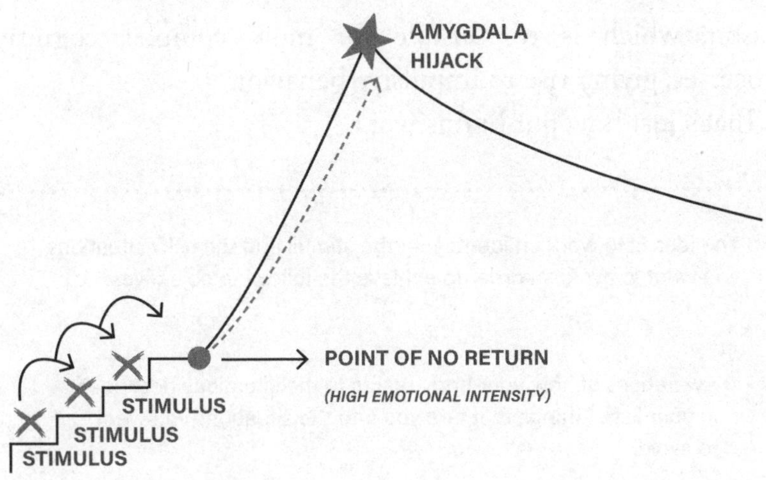

The amygdala, as I mentioned before, is the part of the brain which is mainly responsible for processing and storing emotional reactions. In other words, it's like having another command center in the brain, with the mission of sending out signals giving the green light to impulsive behaviors.

An amygdala hijack is a phenomenon which occurs in the brain when it interprets that it is in a dangerous situation requiring action to survive. As such, although getting back together with your ex in any way is not a life-threatening situation (in principle), in terms of attachment, it is. When it comes to attachment, your brain perceives that if you are not with that person, then you will be alone in the world, and someone alone in the world will barely survive. So, you can imagine what a mess your brain thinks you're in.

Your brain sounds the survival alarm; it considers that it needs to stop processing information and immediately react. To do this, it activates the amygdala, which is responsible for heightened emotions within the brain, and it deactivates reason, which is responsible for more complex cognitive processes, giving rise to impulsive behavior.

That's just how our brains work.

The idea is to work on identifying the stimuli and the risky situations you want to avoid, in order to achieve the following objectives:

- Awareness of how your body reacts to the situations described in your list of things that lure you into the situations you want to avoid.
- Knowledge of what can happen if you react impulsively. In other words, knowing what happens when you "slip" into the "things you want to avoid".
- Prevent negative outcomes and work from a preventative perspective.
- Understand which stimuli cause you to become emotionally dysregulated.
- Avoid exposure to unnecessary stimuli that upset you emotionally.
- Know how to react before acting impulsively or "in the heat of the moment".
- Work on your self-awareness.
- Find possible ways to manage these situations.

You must bear in mind that if you know the stimuli which are likely to tempt you towards the point of no return, and you can identify where that point is, then you will gain an appreciation for where exactly you can't go (this is about knowing your limits). You will also be better able to control your exposure to such stimuli, and emotionally regulate, by using whichever strategies work best for you under the circumstances.

To illustrate this better, let me tell you about Gemma. Gemma was in therapy to stop seeing her ex, whom she had been trying to break up with for over three years. She had tried everything and nothing worked. In one of the sessions, we suggested working on going no contact. At first it worked, but after three weeks Gemma returned to the clinic saying that she had slept with her ex again.

What had happened?

Well, Gemma wasn't applying the no contact rule very well. It turns out that she and her ex still went to the same gym, and when she attempted to implement the no contact rule, she didn't take this small detail into account.

Although she tried to go at different times, he apparently orchestrated a "coincidence" by showing up at the gym at a time when he knew Gemma would be there.

What Gemma told me during the session was that they saw each other and exchanged a few words. Later, she unblocked him on WhatsApp and he took the opportunity to write her a message saying how sorry he was for everything he had done to her. That softened Gemma's heart towards him, and they ended up meeting up.

It was interesting to see how my patient recounted all this, she was really angry with herself, because of course, it wasn't the first time this had happened. Gemma was cool and collected when she told me all of this. But in the heat of the moment, she believed that he really had changed. When she had had time to reflect on it, however, she knew perfectly well that it was all a lie because she'd heard all his excuses so many times before.

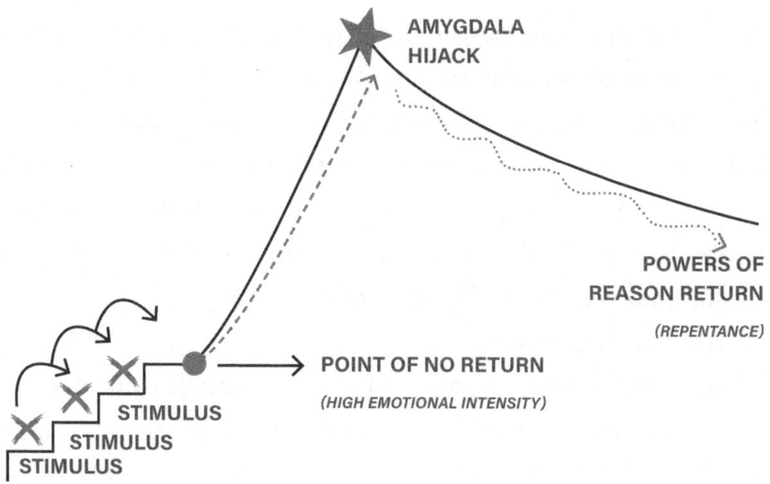

"Gemma," I said, "you have every right to be angry, I understand. But please, don't keep punishing yourself. You already have enough to deal with, battling your emotional dependence. You're not to blame for what happened. Look at what really happened here."

And I gave her the same explanation I'm going to give to you right now:

LET'S SEE HOW MANY *STEPS* HAVE BEEN TAKEN IN THIS STORY:

- **Step 1:** Continuing to go to the same gym as her ex.
- **Step 2:** Talking to her ex at the gym.
- **Step 3:** Unblocking her ex on WhatsApp.
- **Step 4:** Reading the message he sent her.
- **Step 5:** Responding to that message.
- **Step 6:** And point of no return: Meeting up.

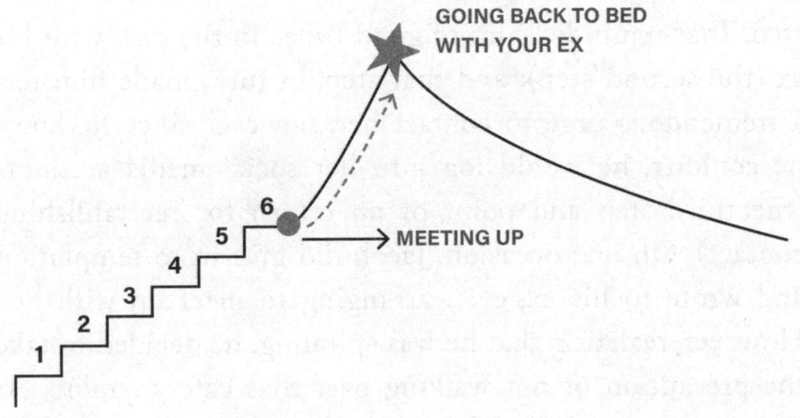

One of the things she most wanted to avoid was going back to bed with him, and this, after going no contact, did not happen by magic. Look at all the steps Gemma climbed without even realizing it. Meeting up was what she predicted would lead to them sleeping together again; however, this could have been prevented if she hadn't taken all those other previous steps, and each step could definitely have been prevented if the previous one hadn't been taken. If Gemma hadn't continued frequenting the same gym as her ex, they probably wouldn't have "bumped into each other", so everything that came after that wouldn't have even happened. Each step makes the next one more likely.

Of course, what I worked on with Gemma in that session was stimulus control, which means controlling the environment and those things which could be identified as potentially leading the person to the point of no return.

Jacob was another patient to whom I applied this theory.

Jacob found it upsetting to frequent a café that he used to go to with his partner. Each day when he went to work in the mornings, he passed the door to the café, saw the sign, and smelled the coffee … he had climbed the first step. That reminded him of good times in the past with his ex (the second step); and that step, in turn, made him feel a tremendous urge to contact her, however since he knew he couldn't, he would log into her social media accounts (the third step and point of no return for reestablishing contact). On one occasion, Jacob did give in to temptation and wrote to his ex, even arranging to meet up with her. However, realizing that he was spiraling, he decided to take the precaution of not walking past that café anymore. At least not for a while. Many years have gone by since then and now, of course, Jacob is perfectly capable of walking past the café again. He even goes there from time to time with his friends for a coffee, with no major repercussions. So, abstinence, beyond the ex-partner, does not have to last forever.

Sometimes we take the first step involuntarily, as in the case of Mark, a patient who recalled his ex via the content of a trivial conversation with a completely different person, unrelated to the relationship.

At the end of the day, all your brain needs is a tiny thread to pull on.

In any case, learning how to slow down the climb is necessary.

When you feel your foot hovering over the first step, it's time to hit the brakes. Yes, you read that right, don't even let yourself reach the second step. You must stop yourself, as soon as you start, because the higher you go, the harder it will be to stop and the more painful the fall.

You could quickly grab a notebook and jot down what you are doing on that first step, how you feel emotionally, noting what you are thinking and feeling in your body.

WHAT AM I DOING?	HOW DO I FEEL?	WHAT AM I THINKING?	WHAT DO I FEEL IN MY BODY?

Once you have jotted down a few answers, see if you can find any repetitive patterns, whether things seem different after you've slept on it, or if you can think of any strategies that might help you to deal with each one.

Next, let me give you a tool that often helps people to regulate their physiological, behavioral, cognitive, and emotional arousal. It's called time out.

In most cases, time out proves to be the most useful technique to help us stop climbing those steps. It's basically "taking a break" or "stepping away from the situation". Just like when you're playing a game and you ask the referee for a time out to leave the court and clear your head.

Time out was originally used with children if they behaved disruptively in class. They were removed from the classroom or whatever environment they were in for a few minutes. Once outside, they were encouraged to take some deep breaths, talk about the situation, and then return to class feeling much calmer. The interesting thing is that this same technique, when used with adults in the situation that's led them to this point, also works well.

HERE ARE SOME EXAMPLES:

- Go for a 20-minute walk.
- If you are at home, go into another room.
- Turn off your phone and put it in a drawer.
- Talk to someone about something else.
- Talk to your therapist.
- Engage in a hobby. For example: Sudokus, word search puzzles, crossword puzzles.
- Count backwards from 100 to 0, subtracting 3 at a time.

If we accompany this with a relaxation technique, such as deep breathing, the benefits are magnified. In my book *Ama tu sexo [Love Your Sex]* you will find lots of strategies to help focus your attention and relax.

I encourage you to give it a try.

WHY DOES THE BREAKUP HURT SO MUCH WHEN WE WERE ONLY TOGETHER FOR A FEW MONTHS?

The key lies in the infatuation stage of falling in love, the phase that precedes "attraction" but comes before "real love", which is precisely the most intense phase of a relationship.

If a relationship ends during the most intense stage, the grief is also more intense and painful because emotionally it is like taking a nosedive. It's like going from 100 to 0 in a very short time, completely taking the wind out of your sails.

Despite what is commonly believed, if the breakup happens during the "real love" phase, the grief is also very painful, but it is not usually experienced as intensely, apart from considering the obvious differences between individuals.

THE PITFALLS OF DEPENDENCE

As if what we've seen so far weren't enough, emotional dependence still has a few more surprises for us in store.

The trap of "feeling like your partner only reacts when faced with losing you"

You need to be especially aware of this particular pitfall of unsuccessful breakup attempts. You know the ones; those moments when you talk to your partner about ending the relationship and they promise they'll change. They do change for a few days, but soon everything slides back to the way it was before.

When someone is pulling away from us, or when we are on the verge of breaking emotional ties, as humans we immediately react to prevent that outcome by giving it our all, however this is not love. It is purely a defense mechanism.

The brain is short-sighted and always looks for the quickest and most effective way to avoid the suffering of a breakup; therefore, its best "weapon" in this situation is to activate this defense mechanism: an intense reaction, expending a lot of energy and throwing everything at the relationship that was previously not being done up until that point, with the intention of maintaining the bond.

Some people do indeed react, change their behavior, and work on making it habitual, to maintain these changes. This is healthy and functional.

Then there are others (the majority) who only change for a few days, later returning to their normal routines and behavior patterns. In the latter case, this pattern of "changing for a short time and returning back to normal" is likely to repeat itself on a never-ending loop.

The trap of "having a final conversation"

Relationships with issues around dependency always feature matters to be resolved and clarified, given their constant swirling uncertainty (do you remember when I said that cognitive dissonance would always be present in relationships like these?). There will always be things left to say. It seems that even after the bond is broken, something still feels like it's "missing", you can never quite seem to draw a line under the relationship, preventing you from feeling at peace. Even if you've broken up, there's always some unresolved issue lurking at the back of your mind, preventing you from fully entering your grief to find peace and tranquility on the other side. For example: "Why did they say they loved me, but then kept ditching me to go out with their friends instead?" "Why did so-and-so tell me that my partner had said something to them, when my partner denied it and said the opposite?"

These creeping doubts make you decide to talk just "one last time" with your partner, to set the record straight and get closure, once and for all. That "last conversation" is the perfect opportunity for you to become hooked again, falling back into the trap of false, dependent love or, in other words, to "try again" for the umpteenth time.

You can't live with these doubts because it's beyond you (I've always felt that uncertainty is the most difficult of all emotions to deal with). So, in that liminal space, fueled by uncertainty and the urgent need to clarify things, full of what-ifs and vulnerability, the other party can take full advantage of the moment to say exactly what they know you need to hear and start manipulating you all over again.

My advice is: don't fall into the trap. You ended the relationship for a reason. Remember your pros and cons list, and keep it close to hand, especially during those first few months of grieving. Focus on your reasons and keep them top of mind. Going back into the fray only makes the problem much bigger than it already is.

QUESTIONS TO ASK YOURSELF WHEN YOU'RE TEMPTED TO GET BACK TOGETHER WITH YOUR EX:

- Am I going back because I really miss my ex, or because I miss the idea of them?
- Do I want to get back into the relationship because I miss my ex, or just because I miss the good times we had?
- Could I experience those positive moments again with someone else in the future, when I feel better and have gotten over the breakup?

- Could my judgement of the relationship be clouded by my refusal to feel the pain of loss?
- Am I going back to my ex out of habit?
- Do I have any real proof that the relationship will change, or is it just wishful thinking that the way I feel about it will change?
- Do I really want to get back together with my ex, or is this decision motivated solely by my fear of loneliness and not finding someone else who will make me happy? (Remember that your happiness does not depend on anyone else.)
- Has anything changed that would make me decide to give the relationship another chance?
- Why would I want to get back together with my ex?
- Is it possible that I miss the plans we made together more than I miss my ex?

When your ex comes back into your life, remember how they make you feel when they leave.

The trap of "emotional numbing"

This particular trap is triggered, once again, by the activation of a defense mechanism in the brain, in the belief that it's the best course of action. (Spoiler alert: it's not.)

As you know, our brain is short-sighted and has a whole set of defense mechanisms at the ready to instantly prevent suffering, even if that means two microseconds of short-lived happiness, followed by long days of discontent. That's why, during the grieving period, when confronted with emotional distress, the brain thinks it's a good idea to spontaneously bring up positive memories of what you experienced together with your ex.

But isn't the best thing for you supposed to be *not* being together with your ex? Of course it is, but right now your brain perceives such intense suffering that it prefers to revel in memories of the good times, feeling good for as long as the memory lasts, rather than persevere through the agony of grief. It doesn't even think about what's coming down the line. And that's the trap. That moment of "emotional numbing", in the form of a good memory, means you've already climbed onto the first step, heading directly to the point of no return if you don't hold back.

"María, the brain is a masochist," a patient of mine once said. Well, it does seem a bit like that, but believe me, it has good intentions. It's not deliberately working against you to mess up your grieving phase or sabotage your attempts to go no contact, quite the opposite, in fact. Your brain thinks it's doing a fantastic job. It would give itself a medal if it could.

The dependent breakup cycle

Almost all of us have fallen into this trap. It is the most common one. The endless loop of "on-again, off-again" dependent relationships. The never-ending push and pull.

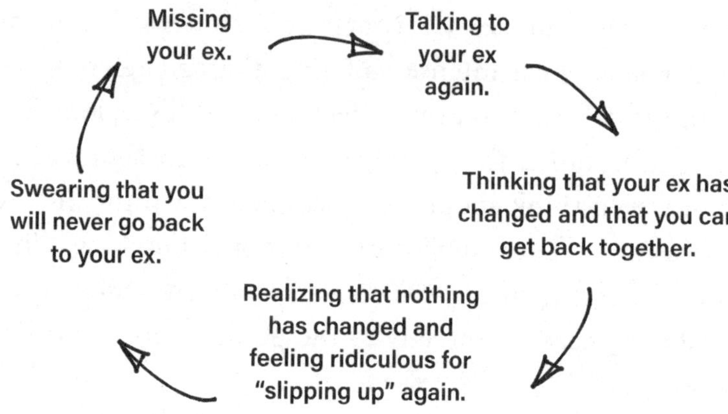

Sounds familiar, right? This cycle can go on for as long as you let it. Gemma spent three years of her life trying to get out of a dependent relationship, just going through this cycle over and over again on repeat.

Rebound relationships

These both are, and are not, part of the breakup. Let me explain.

Rebound relationships are relationships which occur back-to-back, without leaving space in between to grieve the end of the previous relationship.

They are based on questionable clichés such as "in order to get over a man you have to get under a new one." This can be counted as one of those romantic myths because the whole idea behind it is misguided. One person cannot make you forget another. Embarking upon a new relationship or getting excited about someone new doesn't actually help you to process your emotions over the previous breakup. Your grief just gets buried six feet under and left to fester.

When we do this, we're learning to avoid discomfort and to depend upon another person for our own emotional regulation. This is not a healthy approach.

The emotional high of attraction and falling in love with another person squeezes out the thoughts and feelings typical of grief, leaving no room for other emotions. The overall sentiment at this point is one of well-being, but a certain level of dependency may be developing in terms of how you relate to others.

The new partner is essentially "squatting" in the emotional home of the first.

The functional thing to do in this situation would be to stay single during the grieving period, giving time and space over to sadness (and emotions of grief in general) and to reflect, to learn from the experience, and learn how to be alone again. That way, any new relationship can have a healthy start.

I lost count of my rebounds. No one filled the void enough for me to forget the attachment I had to the first one. And it wasn't the fault of the men I met, it was my dependence which was stopping me from turning a new page. I went out with guys, I laughed, I had fun; but I would come home and feel empty. I can't describe it any other way. Something inside me whispered that what I was doing wasn't good for me, and that I should stop, but on the other hand, I needed to feel loved again. So, when the emptiness and the desire to feel wanted set in, I went through my list of contacts and arranged to meet up with someone. Deep down, I desperately wanted to fall in love with that other person. To be honest, I never felt like I was "using" others to get over my breakup. But, of course, now I know that's not how it works.

♥ 10 ♥

ATTACHMENT STYLE

We know that every case is different, and every relationship has its own nuances and particularities; however, thanks to the study of attachment theory in adults, psychologists now have a much easier time analyzing romantic relationships. In order to understand what the dynamics of a relationship are, or will be, we only need to know the attachment style of each person in the relationship.

Psychologist John Bowlby (1977) describes attachment theory as a way of describing the way humans may form strong emotional bonds with others and the various ways of expressing emotions of distress, depression, and anger when they experience unwilling separation or loss. Or, to put it another way, attachment is the way people perceive and respond to intimacy.

According to Bowlby, the type of emotional bond you had with your parents or caregivers has a major influence on your adult relationships.

We could even say that the attachment system, when activated in threatening situations (i.e. situations that the child is unfamiliar with), is responsible for providing a sense of security. When activated, the child seeks out the adult and, depending on the adult's response, the child will continue developing a secure attachment, or alternatively they may end up developing one of the other types: anxious, avoidant, or disorganized attachment.

Let's look at the defining characteristics of each attachment style, based on the relationship the child had with their parents during childhood.

(Before you read on, please know that this information is only intended to help you understand. This knowledge is not meant to justify anything, but simply to lay out a clear explanation. Do not come to your own conclusions and use them to place blame on anyone else's shoulders, as this would be highly unfair. Moreover, without the help of a qualified professional, you could be mistaken in your reasoning. Your parents also carry their own emotional baggage and, although it may be hard to believe, they may have done what they thought was best for you at the time. Also, at times, you have to take into account people's personal characteristics and thought processes. As you well know, some people – for example, those with substance addictions or mental disorders – process things differently due to their individual characteristics.)

SECURE ATTACHMENT

This is associated with the feeling that your parents are stable and can be relied upon. Parents of children who grow up with a secure attachment respond to their children's emotional needs and are perceived by their children as a safe haven. No child with secure attachment is afraid of being abandoned by their parents because, somehow, they know that would be impossible.

With a secure attachment, children can explore, learn about the world, and interact with others, safe in the knowledge that the person with whom they have that attachment bond and whom they consider to be a source of safety, or a safe person (an adult) will be there to protect them. Secure children are children who are upset when separated from their parents but calm down when they are reunited with them.

When this doesn't happen, fears and insecurities influence their interpretation of the world around them, their relationships with other people, and themselves, as you shall see in a moment.

ANXIOUS ATTACHMENT

This attachment style is associated with parents who are sometimes available to their children, but not always. It is related to inconsistency in caregiving behaviors and not always feeling safe.

Faced with such inconsistency, the child understands that their environment lacks stability. This causes them to grow up feeling that the world is a dangerous place (even if nothing bad has ever really happened to them) and that anything can happen at any time (for example, being abandoned). This ultimately makes them fearful and anxious about their environment and insecure in themselves, as their fear, stemming from a belief that the world is too unpredictable, can make them feel unable to cope with it. Children with anxious attachment suffer greatly when separated from their parents and take a long time to calm down when the separation ends.

AVOIDANT ATTACHMENT

This is associated with distant and emotionally unavailable parents.

In terms of self-perception, these children can grow up feeling rejected, unloved, and unworthy.

As a result, the child has no choice but to learn to be self-sufficient. Paradoxically, this makes them appear to others as a child who is confident in themselves and their surroundings, but this behavior is nothing more than a wall they have learned to put up for their own emotional survival.

On the surface, children with avoidant attachment do not seem to suffer or feel pain when their environment changes or if they are separated from their parents (although it has been shown that they do experience stress). This quality is reflected in their tendency to keep some emotional distance from others.

DISORGANIZED ATTACHMENT

This attachment style is a mixture of anxious and avoidant attachment, due to the child's experiences of contradictory and inadequate behavior from their parents.

It is associated with abandonment, neglect, and a level of insecurity in the care and affection they were shown. It is also related to children who have not been taught to respect boundaries and privacy, and who have been the victims of childhood trauma.

Children's risk factors for the development of anything other than secure attachment include being: children who are not listened to, children who are emotionally invalidated, children who are physically or emotionally abused, children who are victims of rape or sexual abuse, children with very demanding parents, overprotected children, children who have overly fearful parents, children who hardly see their parents because they travel or work a lot, children who are unwanted in the family, children with parents who endlessly argue and disrespect each other, children who experience gender-based violence, children whose parents have a psychological disorder or addiction, children whose parents have a totally unbalanced relationship, children who were abandoned at some point in their lives, or children who have experienced a traumatic separation from their parents.

However, it is well known that the quality of care and attention received from parents as a child is not the only contributing factor to our attachment styles as adults. They are conditioned by many other factors too (life experiences, as we saw earlier). This means that a person's history influences the development of their attachment style, and that the characteristics of this style of attachment will be reflected in the way they handle emotional conflicts in relationships.

Therefore, we also see these four types of attachment styles in adults, but they may change due to different experiences at all stages of life. Your attachment style is not set in stone and can vary from when it was formed in childhood. In other words, a person may be born and grow up with a completely secure attachment style, but following a toxic relationship, it may turn into an anxious one. Conversely, someone who initially developed an anxious attachment in their relationship with their parents, thanks to working on themselves and through their life experiences, may find that their attachment style becomes secure. It may also be that someone forms a secure attachment in childhood that remains secure throughout their life, as we saw in previous chapters. Or, as in my case, I grew up with a secure attachment, which changed into an anxious attachment after my first relationship (which was toxic and dependent), and did not change back to a secure attachment until very recently.

Let's see what type of attachment style you identify with as an adult (or young person):

SECURE ATTACHMENT:

- You find it easy to show affection to your partner.
- You enjoy intimacy without worrying excessively about the relationship.
- You feel confident and comfortable being in a relationship, but you also enjoy your own independence and that of your partner.
- You like spending time with your partner, but you also know how to give them space.
- You feel that the love in your relationship is mutual and balanced.
- You are not uncomfortable dealing with emotional conflicts in the relationship and take any issues which may crop up in your stride.
- You know how to communicate your feelings and needs and how to respond to your partner's.
- You are not afraid of abandonment, and you trust in the relationship, but you know that if one day it doesn't work out, you will inevitably have to accept it, however painful that might be.
- You reach out to others when you need support and offer yours when necessary.
- You may have an empathic personality profile.

ANXIOUS ATTACHMENT:

- Relationships tend to take up a large proportion of your emotional bandwidth.
- You tend to worry constantly about the relationship, and consequently your world depends on it.
- You fear that the person you are with does not have the same expectations as you in the relationship, which makes you fear abandonment, causing you to pay excessive attention to small details, such as mood swings, gestures, and behaviors.
- You are very intuitive about other people's attitudes, but you interpret them in such a way that you take things personally. You really struggle with this because it makes you quick to anger. Additionally, you really struggle to control your impulses and tend to mess up easily, although you later regret it and feel guilty.
- You often find yourself looking for problems where there are none; this makes sense, as it is a typical preoccupation for people with an anxious attachment style.
- You show enormous empathy (you may have an empathic personality profile).
- You find it very easy to become intimate and are always seeking emotional intimacy, even if the other person is not yet ready. Sometimes this leads you to believe that your partner doesn't love you as they should.
- You feel miserable when you are not in a relationship.
- You find it very difficult to leave a relationship.
- You suffer greatly when a relationship ends.
- Your desire to form close bonds sometimes drives your partners and potential love interests away.
- You depend heavily on the approval of others and tend to doubt your own worth.
- You tend to idealize your partner.
- You tend to let others set the pace of the relationship.
- During an argument, you feel the need to resolve the conflict immediately. You can't sleep peacefully at night if you and your

partner are still angry with each other.

- If your partner gives you a lot of attention, reassurance, and security, you put your worries aside and feel at ease.
- You tend to be codependent.

AVOIDANT ATTACHMENT:

- You tend to be distant and cold towards others.
- Although you are not afraid of commitment and enjoy intimacy with your partner, you find it overwhelming to do so excessively (which is why you tend to send mixed messages to your partner).
- You find it uncomfortable to be emotionally close to other people or to trust them, so you tend to insist on the importance of setting boundaries.
- People around you often complain that you tend to put emotional or physical distance between yourself and them.
- You find it very difficult to express emotions (saying "I love you" can be a real challenge).
- Talking about emotions, expectations, or the relationship's trajectory is challenging for you.
- Although you can love someone deeply, your partner is not usually your priority.
- Relationships do not cause you much concern, and if one goes wrong, you do not dwell on it for too long.
- You find it very difficult to form emotional intimacy, so most of your relationships tend to be superficial.
- If someone rejects you or hurts you, you tend to withdraw.
- You tend to become defensive at the slightest sign of control or invasion of what you consider your territory by your partner; you value your independence and autonomy highly.
- You tend to idealize your ex-partners, although this does not necessarily mean that you bring your "phantom ex" into your current relationship.
- During an argument, you need to walk away.

DISORGANIZED ATTACHMENT:

- You have love/hate relationships.
- You have explosive reactions to conflict and, even if you manage to approach them calmly, you maintain an aggressive attitude.
- Your relationships are generally full of conflicts, very dramatic, unstable, and emotionally volatile.
- You are extremely afraid of being hurt and of your boundaries not being respected.
- It may sometimes seem that there is no connection between what you do and what you feel.
- On the one hand, you may be afraid of abandonment, but on the other, you find it difficult to be intimate.

I would like to take this opportunity to explain why avoidant attachment can be confused with the narcissistic personality profile. Although these are two different things, people with narcissistic personalities tend to display an avoidant attachment style, however we do also see avoidant people who don't have any narcissistic characteristics at all.

It's not easy to figure out your attachment style. In fact, it is normal to think, "Oh, I'm all of them" or "I'm somewhere in between these two." In my practice, I find out by creating a timeline of the person's history and studying their entire background: family relationships, romantic relationships, friendships, how they have dealt with difficulties in life, studies, work, etc. It's hard to see, but once you do, it suddenly all makes sense. It's usually quite revealing.

A child may grow up with secure attachment, but they may have a toxic and dependent relationship during adolescence that turns their secure attachment into an anxious one. It is also possible to come from having an anxious attachment style, and, after therapy and a healthy relationship, it can be transformed into a more secure one.

It is thought that more than half of the people in the world have a secure attachment style; around 25 percent are avoidant; approximately 20 percent have anxious attachment; and around 3-4 percent have disorganized attachment.

On average, between 70 to 75 percent of adults stay in the same attachment style category their whole lives, while 25-30 percent of the remaining population change their attachment style due to their experiences.

Can your attachment style be changed intentionally? Yes and no. Having secure attachment is like having a treasure; I imagine that no one would want to change it for anything, and certainly not voluntarily. Yes, attachment styles can change, as I mentioned earlier, due to life experiences. Turning any attachment into a secure one, although complicated, is possible. It takes a lot of work on yourself, plus having experiences that echo that personal work, helping to convince our brain that it doesn't have to interpret things the way it does. The average time for a transformation like this is known to take about four years.

It is admittedly difficult to summarize all this theory in just a few pages, and I understand that you may have questions about this information. I will try to tackle any loose ends that might have occurred to you in the simplest way possible.

I am going to focus on the two types of attachment that I consider to be most relevant to the content of this book. Those are anxious and avoidant attachment.

As you will see, they are like night and day. They are the kind of polar opposites which, as we saw at the beginning, do tend to attract. So, as you can imagine, this is a huge problem.

Anxious attachment seeks reassurance in relationships, so, accustomed to being on high alert (in case they are abandoned), the anxiously attached person seeks what they assume will bring them calm reassurance and safety.

Avoidant attachment, given that it has this insurmountable emotional wall or barrier, appears distant and cold. An avoidant person may seem, due to their clear and forceful messages, to have everything very clear (remember that these are people with very firm boundaries). These signals confuse the person with anxious attachment and make them believe that it is a secure attachment. This is usually a completely unconscious process and is largely reflected in our attitudes. In principle, unless, in addition to avoidant attachment, you have a narcissistic personality profile, no one consciously plots these processes as some sort of "emotional trap" for their partner. Not everyone in this life is like Matt, although there are many Matts in this world.

On the other hand, when seeking intimacy, avoidant people focus on those who give them the feeling that, no matter what happens, they will never abandon or reject them, something that anxiously attached people happen to be experts at. And there we have it, the relationship is a ticking time bomb, ready to explode at any moment.

When a person with anxious attachment begins a relationship with an avoidant person, there is fantastic chemistry between the two. Very apt, considering that now we know all about the biochemistry going on behind all the emotional ups and downs, but dependence will also, most likely, feature heavily too.

When conflicts occur, the avoidant person will feel uncomfortable at the mere suggestion of emotionally confronting the situation and will retreat back into their "cave", while the anxious person will desperately engage in protest behaviors in an attempt to get the avoidant's attention (they will follow them around, desperately trying to solve the problem), which is likely to overwhelm the avoidant person even more.

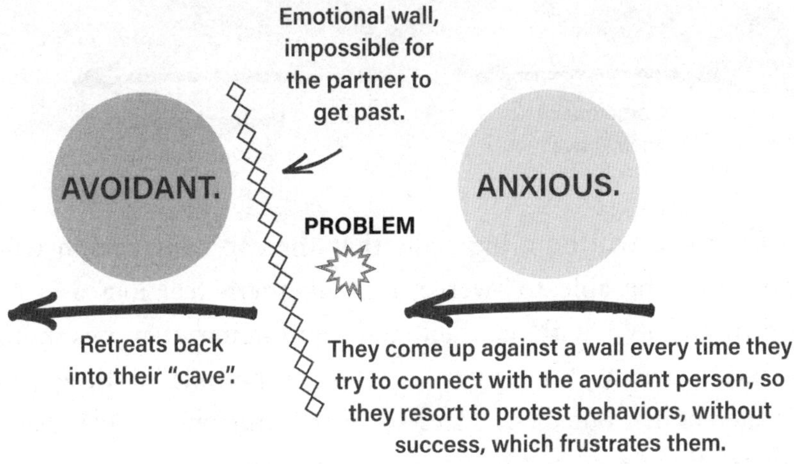

When the avoidant person has cooled off, they return "as if nothing happened", however for the anxious person, they will be completely on edge, because while the avoidant person was in their "cave", the anxious person was left alone with their thoughts, turning everything over and over in their minds, non-stop. This, as you can imagine, is the perfect opportunity for the brain to start coming up with all its own interpretations of events, filling in the gaps, anticipating, catastrophizing and carrying out other typical cognitive activities. When the avoidant person approaches the anxious person again in attempts to reestablish the normal routine, two things can happen:

Either the anxious person will protest ("I don't want to talk right now"; which means "I'm angry and feel like I can't breathe").

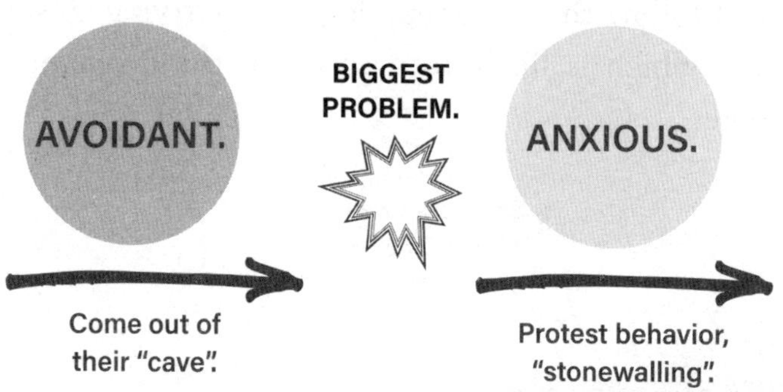

Or there will be a big fight that the avoidant person will no longer be able to swerve, making them feel increasingly uncomfortable with conflict and reinforcing that desire to avoid problems for longer and longer periods of time (no longer hours, but days). And so, every time the couple clash, we see this never-ending pattern repeat itself.

Now there is no longer conflict, there is real fighting and resentment. Combative attitudes. Both will complain about a lack of empathy and understanding from the other.

Given this explanation, my patients always ask me if this dynamic can be changed and how to do so.

Well, human beings almost always have enough neural plasticity to contemplate the possibility of change, but I will be honest: there are times when such change is extremely complicated and almost impossible to work on. Even taking into account each person's personal characteristics, if there is already a pattern of toxic behavior in the relationship (behaviors such as those discussed in previous chapters), and this has been sustained over time, with resentment building up in the relationship, it is very, very difficult to change the dynamic, as each person in the couple has already been consistently learning these patterns in terms of how they relate to one another.

That said, if each person in the couple, and the relationship in general, appears open and amenable to change, then all it would take is simply gaining more insight into each other, combined with implementing some key strategies, for both people to feel emotionally stable in the relationship (something we already know is important for feeling safe and secure, even when things are going downhill):

- The avoidant person must clearly communicate to let their partner know that they are unable to deal with the situation at that particular moment (remember the 24-hour rule). That way, the anxious person can relax, with none of the sense of "abandonment" which would be more typical in this type of scenario.
- The anxious person must learn to manage their thoughts and interpretations of things, while the avoidant person remains in their "cave" so as not to make the problem bigger than it already is.

- When the avoidant partner comes out of their "cave" and returns, they should be willing to talk about the problem. This shows that they care about the problem and just needed some time to gather their thoughts and manage their feelings.
- The anxious partner, far from protesting, must also be willing to establish effective communication strategies to address the problem, without bringing up the past or flinging accusations around.
- If both parties can maintain this approach to problems, then they will be acting as a team and, in turn, forging a more stable and secure relationship.

In terms of personal characteristics, the avoidant person may also have what's known as "Peter Pan syndrome" (very common in this personality profile).

PETER PAN SYNDROME:

- Need for admiration.
- Superficial relationships.
- Their partners tend to take on the role of parent, psychologist, or nurse.
- They are very demanding in their relationships.
- They see commitment as an obstacle to freedom.
- They attribute negative things to external factors. They do not take responsibility for their actions. They pass the buck.
- They feel misunderstood.
- They are only focused on themselves.
- They are non-conformists, but not productive.
- They are insecure and have low self-esteem.

- They are unable to mature (they have no desire to "grow up" or take on responsibilities beyond those imposed on them, such as at work).
- This is common in men.

As a result, the anxious profile will end up developing Wendy syndrome, thereby creating codependency with the person who has the avoidant profile.

WENDY SYNDROME:

- Usually develops in codependent people.
- They have an overwhelming need to satisfy their partner.
- They are people who tend to make themselves small in the relationship.
- They feel a need to please their partner.
- They constantly seek acceptance from others.
- They fear rejection or feeling that no one loves them.
- They believe that if they take care of the other person, that person will not abandon them.
- The person feels essential; they believe that without them, the other person would be unable to cope.
- They tend to conceive of love as a "sacrifice".
- They tend to be submissive.
- They overprotect their partner to such an extent that they put the partner before themselves.
- They internalize problems and negative things. They take the blame. They always consider themselves responsible and/or guilty.
- They tend to act as a mother/father, psychologist, and nurse towards their partner.
- Common in women.

People with anxious personality profiles are very prone to the erroneous belief that they have the power to change their partner ("I'll make them change" or "I'm sure their love for me will make them change"). This makes them the perfect target for people who play the "I want to change, but I just need your help" game.

For me, the most important things when it comes to knowing what type of attachment each person has are:

- **Paying attention to their attitudes.** I pay much more attention to what people show me through their actions than what they put into words. I ask myself, "If this person were mute right now, what would their attitude towards the relationship be demonstrating to me?"
- **Being able to clearly identify what they are looking for in the relationship.** "Let's not put a label on it" is not a valid answer for me. I think it's fine to go with the flow, but I think it's even better to have a clear "why".
- **Looking for several attachment style characteristics without narrowing in on just one.** This gives me a rough idea of their attachment style. If you have a good understanding of attachment theory, you can intuit this sooner rather than later, but if not, it's not until a few months later that you see it clearly (when the infatuation phase ends and the disappointment phase begins).
- And, most importantly, I pay a great deal of attention to **how they react to effective communication.** I'm not afraid to bring up emotionally charged topics in conversation to see how they handle them. If I bring up a sensitive topic and they react defensively, that's good intel for me. If their reaction is to tiptoe around the issue, that's also good information. If they react by ignoring me, again, that's information. And if they react with active listening and empathy, that tells me a lot too. It's all information. Occasionally a patient will say to me, "I feel uncomfortable talking about this," to which I respond, "You'll feel even more uncomfortable when you have no choice but to bring it up and you find their reaction disappointing (if that's the case)."

♥ 11 ♥

HEALTHY RELATIONSHIPS

Throughout this book, I have given you quite a few clues on how to build healthy relationships, but to make it crystal clear and give you a good reference guide to follow, I am going to lay out a few pointers on what it means to have a healthy and functional bond.

HEALTHY RELATIONSHIPS FEATURE MOST OF THE FOLLOWING CHARACTERISTICS:

- The feeling of being "at peace" is constant and unwavering.
- You both go to bed at night knowing that you will love each other just as much the next day.
- Even if you clash sometimes, your relationship never falters because you take advantage of the opportunity to talk and find solutions as a team.
- You end the conversation when you know it's going nowhere.
- You never see each other as enemies.
- You take full responsibility for your own mistakes.
- You apologize whenever the other person feels hurt, regardless of whether you think they are right or not, because you show empathy and understand that you may perceive things differently.
- You do not constantly seek demonstrations of loyalty or commitment.
- You are trustworthy and consistent in your actions.
- You are sincere, without being brutally honest.
- You maintain respectful privacy with things like your emails, social media, and passwords, because you understand that sharing this type of information with the other person is unnecessary.
- The household chores are divided up between yourselves based on what you are best at and enjoy doing most (and if you are not good at something, or you don't enjoy it, you do it anyway, because it remains a chore that still needs to be done).

- You are each other's top priority, but don't neglect your respective lives as individuals either.
- You can always count on each other.
- You always find each other supportive and ready to listen.
- You are not afraid to address conflicts; however, you do understand that some issues can be more difficult to confront than others, which may make you feel nervous to face them.
- You are not just a couple; you're also best friends.
- You do lots of things together, but also individually.
- You still go on dates, even if you live in the same house, because you know that boredom can set in over time, and that too much routine will take its toll.
- You devote time to keeping the spark alive and rekindling affection in your relationship.
- You kiss, hug, and tell each other you love each other all the time (whenever possible, of course).
- Sexuality in the relationship is treated as just one more way, among others, to nurture affection, and is not used as a bargaining chip.
- The relationship is reciprocal.
- Every day, you choose each other as partners, freely and willingly.
- You don't feel chained down by each other.
- You don't feel that the relationship is constrictive.
- You celebrate each other's achievements, no matter what they are.
- You encourage each other to grow as individuals and work together to make sure that happens.
- You are not scared of suddenly being abandoned because you know that if one day the other person's feelings towards the relationship change, they will communicate this clearly to you, without hesitation.
- You understand that the relationship can change and evolve.
- You feel secure.

- If either one of you feels jealous, you calmly discuss it together, as many times as needed.
- When either party is feeling down, you set aside time and space to talk about it.
- You keep your promises.
- You are not afraid that your partner might one day let you down over plans made together.

It doesn't surprise me that there are people who, when feeling calm within a relationship, might mistake that calm for boredom or a lack of love, instead of considering that they have simply found emotional stability with someone. That's what happened to me. Since I've recounted many experiences from my own love life throughout this book, I'd like to talk about my current relationship.

In my case, after six years with my current partner, Alberto, and after doing a lot of work on myself, I've come to see the silver linings of my experiences. They've helped me to grow as a person and learn exactly what I want and need in a relationship, as well as what I don't. I would go so far as to say that if I hadn't had those experiences, as dramatic as this might sound, I would never have even imagined that what I have now was even the tiniest possibility.

And while it's true that in this book I have focused more on the most negative experiences, I must say that I was also lucky enough to meet people with whom I had a healthy bond, but which I mistook for a lack of interest, which is why those relationships didn't work out.

Everything changes when you see things from a different perspective. And learning helps you see everything differently. Personally, I have learned a lot:

- I have learned that where there is suffering, there is no love.
- I have learned what it means to treat others with respect and to be treated with respect myself.
- I have learned that in order to love someone in a healthy way, I first have to love myself.
- I have learned that I must put myself first.
- I have learned that my partner also has to be my best friend.
- I have learned that if I feel unable to talk to my partner about even the tiniest of my concerns (when previously it was something I felt comfortable doing), then I will feel uneasy and unable to be myself.
- I have learned that material possessions do not matter at all if there is no love.
- I have learned that I need to have hobbies in common with my partner.
- I have learned that even though I might be afraid to tell my partner what I think or feel, I must do so because, regardless of how they react, it will tell me a lot about how they personally handle things themselves.
- I have learned that I don't always have to give in to make the other person happy.
- I have learned that I must set strong boundaries about things that I don't like, or which hurt me.
- I have learned that I can handle anything, but that it's true that you can bring a horse to water, but you can't make it drink.
- I have learned that not everything depends on me.
- I have learned that relationships must be reciprocal.
- I have learned that trying tirelessly is never enough if the other person doesn't show any genuine desire or commitment.

- I have learned that feeling like you're on an emotional roller coaster in a relationship is not healthy.
- I have learned that I had relationships that do not deserve to be called such because I was the only one who was committed.
- I have learned that if someone loves you, they will seek out your company.
- I have learned that no matter how many "highs" they give me, if there is any hint of mixed signals, it is not worth it.
- I have learned that when times get tough, I need to feel my partner is there for me.
- I have learned that if someone makes me feel worthless, I must run in the opposite direction!
- I have learned that I hate lying, because I know what it feels like to be lied to over and over again.
- I have learned that I need someone by my side who loves to travel, learn about other cultures, and who has an insatiable curiosity to learn about absolutely everything.
- I've learned that I don't need to "mother" my partner, and not to shoulder their responsibilities as if they were my own.
- I have learned that feeling sexually liberated goes far beyond just having orgasms.
- I have learned that where desire and interest collide, there is no such thing as repeatedly hearing "Oh no, I can't today" all the time.
- I have learned that serious conversations should never take place via instant messaging.
- I have learned that others will not respect me unless I demonstrate that I have self-respect first.
- I have learned to be comfortable single.
- I have learned that being in a relationship is much more than just meeting up occasionally and having sex.
- I have learned that having a partner is much more than just not being single.

- I have learned that it is better for a partner to share in my own happiness than for them to feel somehow obliged to "make me" happy. My emotions are my own responsibility, and it is better not to put them in anyone else's hands.
- I have learned not to put expectations on others.
- I have learned not to demand perfection from myself.
- I have learned to let go.
- I have learned to be myself.

Thanks to all of this, six years ago I was able to experience healthy love, real love, the kind I would never trade for any of those past traumatic relationships, but for which, paradoxically, the traumas were a necessary part of the journey to get me where I am today.

I am sure that my relationship with him has been a key factor in changing the way I relate to myself and others. Seeing my dysfunctional learning about relationships reflected in my relationship with him and not receiving any kind of reinforcement from him (quite the opposite, in fact) made me question the relationship model I had had up until then. With him, I never engaged in protest behavior because he never gave me any reason to do so, and if at any point my mind started playing tricks on me, he was there to listen and help assuage my fears of being abandoned again.

From the day I first met him, I could feel that peace of mind I've been talking about. I won't deny that at first it felt strange. "Maybe he doesn't like you or doesn't like you enough," I thought. But just this once, I decided to let myself take the chance. After all, what could possibly go wrong that hadn't already happened to me? Another disappointment? I was overprepared for whatever came my way.

That initial feeling of calm, so different from the kind of rush I was used to, was what made me take the leap with him.

Alberto was different to anyone I had ever met before. He was decent and approachable. He wasn't a man who came to "save me" with the emotional stability I imagined he had. He actually demonstrated it. He wasn't a riddle for me to figure out. He didn't make me feel uncertain. I didn't have to be on high alert in case he left me for another girl. He didn't play games by not answering, and if I did, due to my own bad habits (you know, the emotional baggage, the trauma), he continued to show me affection. Just showing me affection and interest like that, at times when I had expected him to slope off and disappear like the others, initially really threw me off balance. Which is tragic really, isn't it? There comes a point where we get so used to being treated badly in relationships that when we are treated well, it seems odd.

Sometimes, when I talk about healthy relationships at work, during my counseling sessions or outreach, and I explain what they are, some people think I'm presenting an idealized or romanticized view of relationships, but that's not the case at all. What's romanticized in our society is everything that isn't a healthy relationship. And, strange as it may seem, what we might imagine as the "ideal" relationship is what should actually be the norm.

Alberto, despite having a secure attachment style, found some of those relationship skills that just have to be learned, unfamiliar territory. He had to pick them up as he went along. Back then, and in fact as we continue to do now, we both worked hard for the relationship to be successful.

And next year we're getting married! Wow.

Forgive me, but it feels strange to write that down. It's as if I'm suddenly much more aware of the step we're about to take. I still remember our first date. I can't believe everything I've had to go through to get here. You'd be right in thinking it hasn't been easy.

In my past, I knew what I wanted, but not what I didn't want.

Over the years, I've learned to be more aware of what I went through in the past. I've learned to love and value myself, first and foremost as a person, and then as a partner. I think that perhaps this level of personal growth is actually my life's greatest accomplishment. Sometimes I do have some intrusive bad memories, but there's one thing I'm very proud of, and that is that I've learned to deal with them and be at peace with myself.

Although I know that in the past I didn't do things the way I would have liked to do them now, it wasn't my fault that things turned out the way they did; I simply didn't know any better.

Self-acceptance is a key part of the hard work of self-forgiveness.

And it is my sincere hope, dear reader, that you will be able to forgive yourself one day too.

BIBLIOGRAPHY

ANGULO EGEA, M. (2009). «¿Crecer? Nunca jamás. Peter Pan y Wendy: dos patrones de conducta adolescente». *La Torre Del Virrey* , *1* (6, 2009/1), 105-113. Source: https://revista. latorredelvirrey.es/LTV/article/view/698

ANICAMA, J. (2014). Tratamiento cognitivo-conductual de la ansiedad. Fobias. Seminar: «Aprende de los mejores». ISEP. Madrid.

BOWLBY, J. (1977). *The making and breaking of affectional bonds. The British Journal of Psychiatry,* 130(3): 201-210.

CONGOST, S. (2020). *Si duele no es amor. Aprende a identificar y a liberarte de los amores tóxicos.* Barcelona: Editorial Planeta.

CONGOST, S. (2015). *Cuando amar demasiado es depender. Aprende a superar la dependencia emocional.* Barcelona: Editorial Planeta.

ESCLAPEZ, M. (2017). *Inteligencia sexual. Desarrolla tu potencial sexual, practica sexo inteligente.* Almuzara. Madrid: Arcopress Ediciones.

ESCLAPEZ, M. (2020). *Ama tu sexo.* Barcelona: Bruguera. Penguin Random House Grupo Editorial.

ETXEBARRÍA, L. (2013). *Tu corazón no está bien de la cabeza.* Barcelona: Paidós Ibérica. Editorial Planeta.

GAJA, R. (2005). *Vivir en Pareja.* Barcelona: Debolsillo. Random House Mondadori.

GRAY, J. (2013*) Men are from Mars, Women are from Venus GRAY, J. (2013). Los hombres son de Marte, las mujeres son de Venus.* Barcelona: Grijalbo. Random House Mondadori.

HERNÁNDEZ, M. (2017). *Apego y Psicopatología. La ansiedad y su origen.* Bilbao: Desclée De Brouwer.

HOGENBOOM, M. (2016). «Las siniestras razones por las que nos enamoramos». Source:noticias/2016/02/160219_vert_earth_siniestra_razon_enamoramos_yv

LEVINE, A., y HELLER, R. (2016). *Maneras de amar. La nueva ciencia del apego adulto y cómo puede ayudarte a encontrar el amor . . . y conservarlo.* Barcelona: Ediciones Urano.

MANRIQUE MUÑANTE, R. (2013). «El amor: hay (bioquímica entre nosotros». *Revista de Química,* 27(1-2), 29-32. Source: https://revistas.pucp.edu.pe/index.php/quimica/ article/view/8968

NACIONES UNIDAS *[United Nations].* «¿Qué es el maltrato en el hogar?». Consulted in 2021. Source: https://www.un.org/es/coronavirus/what-is-domestic-abuse

PUNSET, E. (2005) «La intuición no es irracional». RTVE. Source: https://www.rtve.es/play/videos/redes/redes-intuicion-no-irracional/5427256/

SAIZ, M. (2015). «La feniletilamina del amor». *Independientes, Revista especializada en adicciones*. Source: http://revistaindependientes.com/la-feniletilamina-del-amor/

QUIJADA, P (2013). «El cerebro enamorado». Source: https://abcblogs.abc.es/cosas-cerebro/curiosidades/el-cerebro- enamorado.html

RUIZ, L. «¿Cuánto dura el enamoramiento?». *Psicología y mente*. Consulted in 2021. Source: https://psicologiay-mente.com/pareja/cuanto-dura-enamoramiento

VÁZQUEZ, C. (2020). «Pareidolia: ¿por qué vemos formas conocidas en los objetos?». Source: https://www.eldiario.es/consumoclaro/cuidarse/pareidolia-vemos-formas-conocidas- nubes_1_5967577.html

ABOUT THE AUTHOR

María Esclapez is a psychologist, author, and public speaker with expertise in clinical psychology, sexology, and couples therapy. Her bestselling books on relationships, emotional intelligence, and personal growth have sold over 250,000 copies internationally.

María is based in Elche, Spain.

---

mariaesclapez.com
Instagram: @maria_esclapez
TikTok: @maria_esclapez
Threads: @maria_esclapez